GARDEN PROJECTS
for the
BACKYARD CARPENTER

Tina Skinner

Schiffer Publishing Ltd

4880 Lower Valley Road, Atglen, PA 19310 USA

D1400030

Designed by Bonnie M. Hensley
Type set in CopprplGoth Bd BT/Lydian BT

ISBN: 0-7643-1234-0
Printed in China

Published by Schiffer Publishing Ltd.
4880 Lower Valley Road
Atglen, PA 19310
Phone: (610) 593-1777; Fax: (610) 593-2002
E-mail: Schifferbk@aol.com
Please visit our web site catalog at
www.schifferbooks.com

This book may be purchased from the publisher.
Include $3.95 for shipping. Please try your bookstore first.
We are always looking for people to write books on new and related
subjects. If you have an idea for a book please contact us at the above
address.
You may write for a free catalog.

In Europe, Schiffer books are distributed by
Bushwood Books
6 Marksbury Avenue
Kew Gardens
Surrey TW9 4JF England
Phone: 44 (0) 20-8392-8585; Fax: 44 (0) 20-8392-9876
E-mail: Bushwd@aol.com
Free postage in the UK. Europe: air mail at cost.

TABLE OF CONTENTS

FOREWORD

This book was made possible by three organizations that supplied images and plans: Georgia-Pacific Corporation, Southern Pine Council, and the California Redwood Association.

Provided are plans for 33 do-it-yourself backyard projects. Enough to fill any backyard, and any handyman's schedule for several spring seasons. These projects were chosen for their ability to enhance outdoor living, creating a better environment for our families as well as a few furry and feathered friends.

It is important, after choosing a project, that you read the complete instructions before beginning work or purchasing materials and tools. Neither Schiffer Publishing, Ltd., Georgia-Pacific Corporation, Southern Pine Council, nor the California Redwood Association make any warranties expressed or implied regarding these plans.

Woodworking Do's and Don'ts

Before beginning any home remodeling project, check with your local building department to learn if a permit is required and to discover any special building codes for your locality. Check with an architect or a building expert to make sure that this plan is appropriate to your situation.

Remember, safety comes first. The use of standard safety equipment reflects good common sense. Eye protection, dust mask, and gloves should be used when sawing or machining any type of building material, including wood products, treated or untreated. Practicing good personal hygiene at the completion of any construction project also applies.

Sawing should be done outdoors while wearing a dust mask. Eye goggles should also be worn when power sawing or machining.

When nailing toward the ends of lumber pieces, blunt the nail points or pre-drill the holes to avoid splitting.

Use hot-dipped galvanized or stainless steel fasteners and hardware for all connections to prevent rust damage.

Using Treated Lumber

The Southern Pine Council recommends that you use treated Southern Pine material with a preservative retention of .40 for applications in contact with the ground. Retentions of .25 are for above-ground applications.

Clothing accumulating sawdust from treated wood products should be laundered before re-use and washed separately from other household clothing. Areas of skin in contact with treated wood should be thoroughly washed before eating, drinking, or using tobacco products.

Treated wood scraps should be disposed of by ordinary trash collection; they should not be burned.

For additional information on treated Southern Pine, contact the Southern Pine Council at Box 641700, Kenner, LA 70064.

Buying Treated Lumber

Radius Edge Decking, R.E.D., is a popular Southern Pine product that's perfect for most decking applications. In lumber terminology, R.E.D. is "five-quarter" or 5/4 material. Actual (dressed) thickness is 1". Nominal widths are available, with 4" and 6" widths most commonly available. Each piece features a founded edge (-1/4" radius) that provides comfortable seating and walking surfaces. R.E.D. can span a maximum of 24", though many builders typically use 16" on center spacing for deck joists for less springiness.

G-P Plus and Southwoods Collection and Sturd-I-Floor are registered trademarks of Georgia-Pacific Corporation.

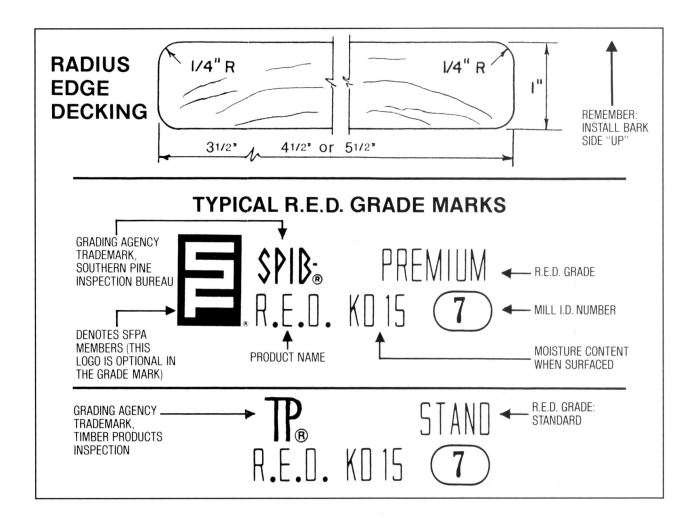

Using Redwood

When using untreated lumber, redwood is naturally superior to other woods for outdoor applications: it shrinks and swells less than other woods and is less likely to warp, split, check, or cup. With little or no pitch, redwood is easy to drill, saw, and shape. Redwood heartwood has natural durability and resistance to insects and will last longer outdoors than most woods.

The knotty garden grades of redwood are ideal for outdoor projects. These grades are beautiful, durable, and economical.

Construction Heart/Deck Heart is all heartwood and contains knots. It is used for load-bearing applications near the ground. Deck Heart is graded for strength and is available in 2x4 and 2x6.

Construction Common/Deck Common contains sapwood and knots. It is used for decking and above-ground uses. Deck Common is graded for strength and is available in 2x4 and 2x6.

Merchantable Heart is all heartwood and contains larger knots than Construction grades. It is used near the soil.

Merchantable contains sapwood and larger knots. It is used for fence boards, rails, and above-ground uses.

Finishes for Redwood

Redwood accepts finishes better than most woods. Some heighten redwood's natural beauty, bringing out the color and the grain. Others help the wood harmonize or contrast with surrounding structures. Keep in mind that unfinished redwood will gradually turn soft driftwood gray. Read the labels on all finish products before using.

* Clear water-repellent finish is recommended to stabilize the color at tan.

* Semi-transparent stains in "redwood" shades tint the wood without hiding the grain.

* Solid-color stains or paints should be applied over compatible oil-based primers.

Adhesives for Treated Wood

New construction adhesives, specially formulated for joining pressure-treated wood, are now available in caulk-type dispensers. The new adhesives are not a replacement for nailing, but they do strengthen joints and add durability to the finished project.

Finishes for Treated Lumber

Although pressure-treated Southern Pine is protected against mold, mildew, and termite attack, the application of a water-repellent sealer is recommended once construction is complete. This sealer, formulated for use on treated wood, will help control surface checking and provide an attractive appearance.

GALLERY

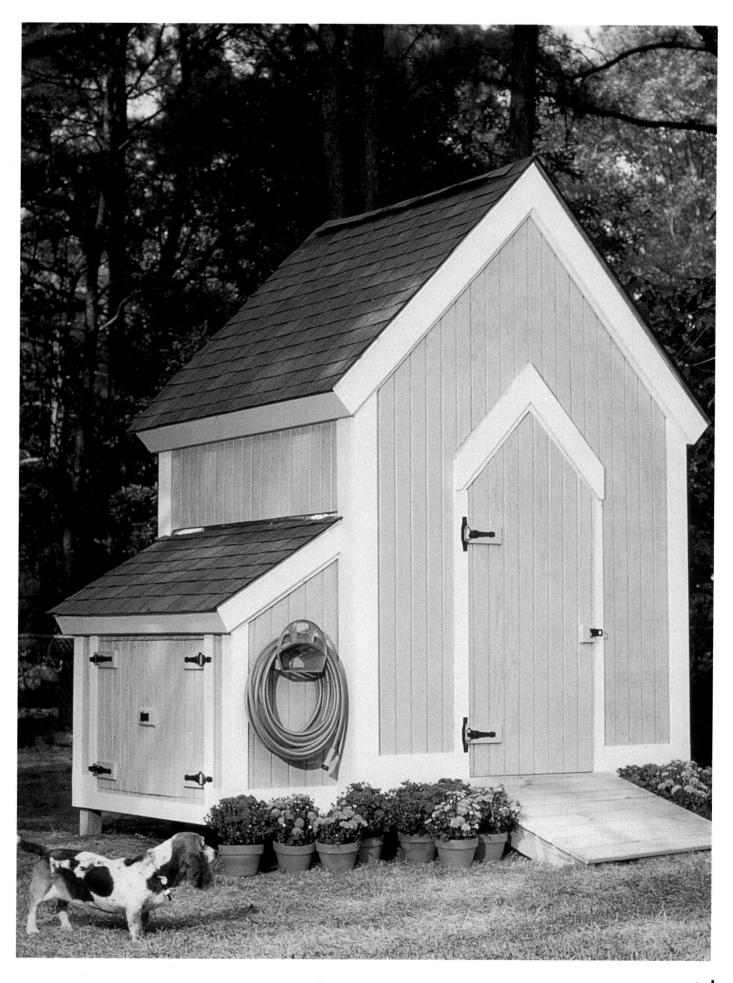

Flush-Top 4x4 Redwood Planter

Courtesy of the California Redwood Association

This handsome planter will enliven a deck, garden, or patio. For best results, the California Redwood Association recommends that you measure and trim each piece as you build. Pre-drill holes, especially at the ends of boards, to prevent splitting. Use only top-quality, hot-dipped galvanized nails to prevent stains.

Materials

Ground-contact Wood

4	4x4s at 15 inches
16	1x4s at 22-1/2 inches
4	2x6s at 22-1/2 inches
2	2x4s at 24-1/2 inches

Common Wood

16	1x4s at 22-1/2 inches
4	1x4s at 26-1/2 inches
8	2x2s at 15 inches

Other

60	12-penny nails
160	6-penny nails
Polyethylene liner	

Instructions

1. Nail two 2x2s to adjacent faces of each 4x4 corner post. Use 12d nails. Leave room for the 1x4 panels to fit flush with outer faces of the 4x4 posts.
2. Attach 1x4 boards to posts with two 6d nails at each board end. The 1x4 boards should be evenly spaced along the post and flush with the bottom and outer face. Use construction heart (ground-contact wood) for interior walls.
3. Complete two walls, both inside and out, to form an "L" as shown in the illustration. Then construct the last two walls, completing the box. It may help to lay the project on its side when nailing the last walls.
4. For the base, turn the box upside down and place 2x4s on opposite sides, one inch in from the edge. With two 12d nails in each board end, attach the 2x4s to the 4x4 posts. Drill two 1-inch drainage holes in two of the 2x6s to be used for the bottom. Turn the box upright and lay all four 2x6s in place to form the bottom of the planter.
5. For the top trim, butt-join 1x4s flush with the planter's outer edge. Use two 6d nails at each board end, penetrating the 4x4 at one end and the 2x2 at the other. These nails can be countersunk and filled with non-oily wood filler.
6. Interior surfaces should be lined with a polyethylene liner. Make sure to provide proper drainage by cutting holes through the bottom of the planter and the liner.

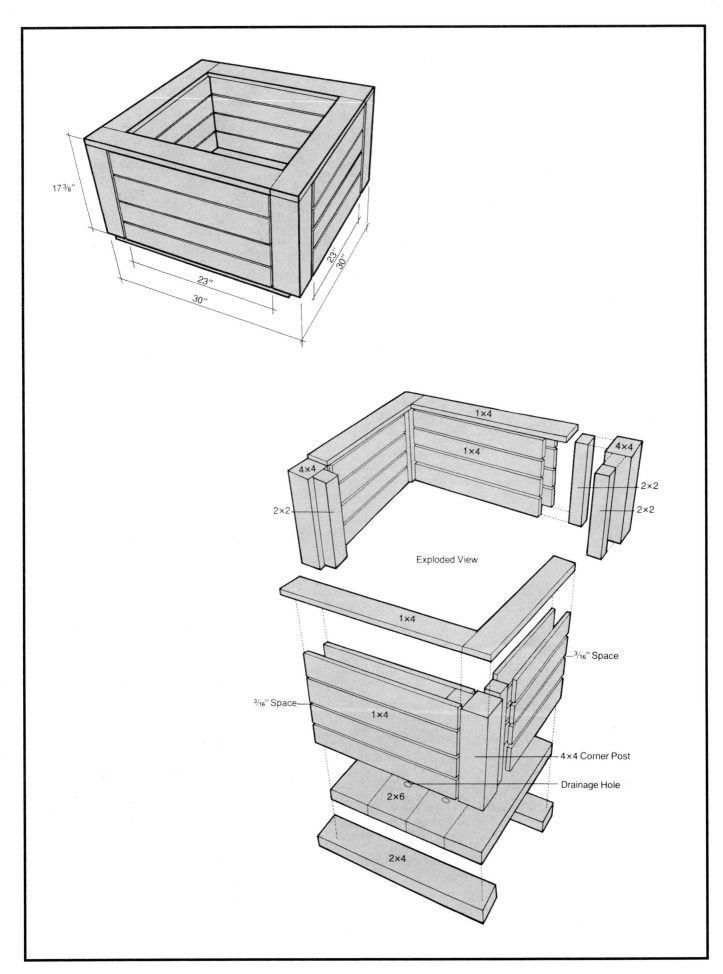

17 3/8"

30"

23"

23"

30"

1×4

1×4

4×4

4×4

2×2

2×2

2×2

2×2

Exploded View

1×4

3/16" Space

3/16" Space

1×4

4×4 Corner Post

Drainage Hole

2×6

2×4

Courtesy of the California Redwood Association

3x3 Planter with Corner Posts

A decorative planter box can be an impressive accent to your deck or patio. Along with a few tools and some hardware, this plan from Southern Pine Council will take you step-by-step through the complete construction of your new planter box. When you complete it, add your choice of greenery and flowers, sit back, relax, and admire your new addition to your outdoor living area.

Courtesy of Southern Pine Council

Materials

Wood

1	4x4 at 10 feet
1	2x6 at 12 feet
4	2x4 at 6 feet
1	2x4 at 8 feet
10	1x4s at 6 feet

Other

6d and 10d hot-tipped nails
2 sheets polyethylene film, approximately 41 x 73 inches
Construction adhesive for pressure-treated lumber.
Water-repellent sealer

Instructions

1. Cut wood as follows:

    a. From the 4x4 cut four pieces 29 inches long. Referring to the plan, make the appropriate cuts for the decorative corner post design.

    b. From the 2x6, use a miter box at 45 degrees and cut 4 pieces 36 inches long.

    c. From the 6-foot 2x4s cut eight pieces 33 inches long.

    d. From the 8-foot 2x4 cut two pieces 26 inches long; one piece 33 inches long.

    e. From the 1x4 material use the miter box at 45 degrees and cut 20 pieces 31 inches long. Save the scraps.

2. Using 10d nails, attach two 33-inch 2x4 cross members to the 2x6 base, 12" on center as shown in the plan. Make sure one edge of each 2x4 rests flush with one edge of the 2x6.

3. Complete the base frame by attaching the other two 2x6 members using construction adhesive and two 10d nails

per mitered corner joint.

4. Attach the 4x4 corner posts to the 2x6 base frame members using 10d nails and construction adhesive.

5. Complete the base decking with seven 33-inch 2x4s and two 26-inch 2x4s using 10d nails.

6. Drill two 3/8-inch deep holes in each of the 2x4 decking members, as shown in the plan.

7. Attach 1x4 side panel boards to the 4x4 posts as shown in the plan, starting the bottom board flush with the 2x6 base. Use construction adhesive and two 6d nails at each board end. Remember to either pre-drill the holes or blunt nail points to avoid splitting the 1x4 boards.

8. Use a razor knife to cut the poly film according to the pattern on the plan. Form the poly film liner inside the box by overlapping the two sheets. Fold over the top four or five inches of film to form a double-layer flap. Using leftover 1x4 pieces as tacking blocks, sandwich the liner between the 1x4 blocks and one inch below the top lip of the planter. Nail to the 4x4 posts using 6d nails. Repeat in all four corners. Puncture the liner bottom to allow moisture to pass through the weep holes.

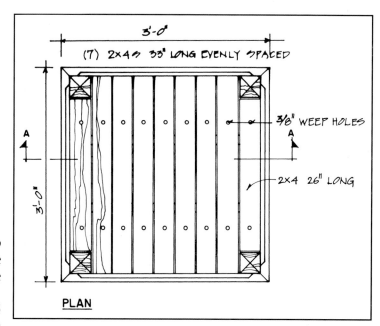

Courtesy of Southern Pine Council

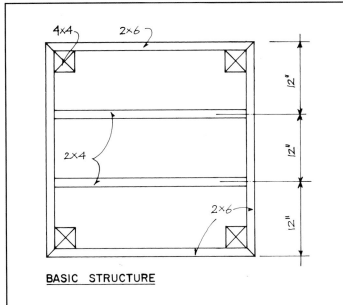

BASIC STRUCTURE

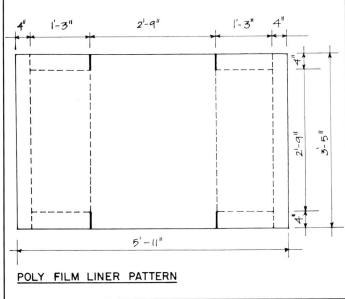

POLY FILM LINER PATTERN

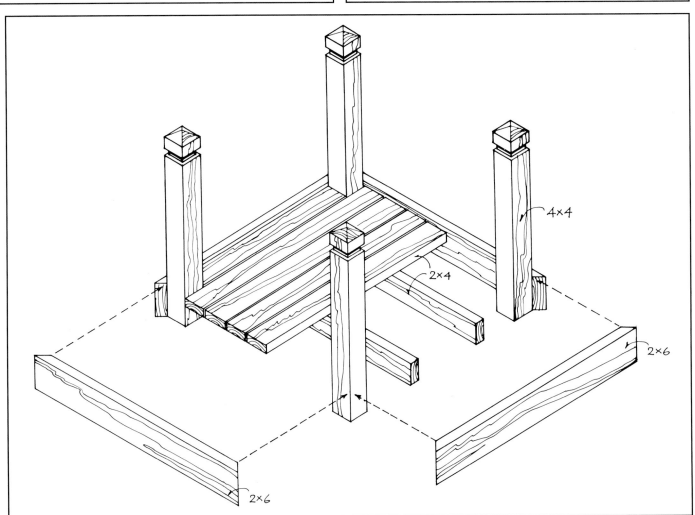

Courtesy of Southern Pine Council

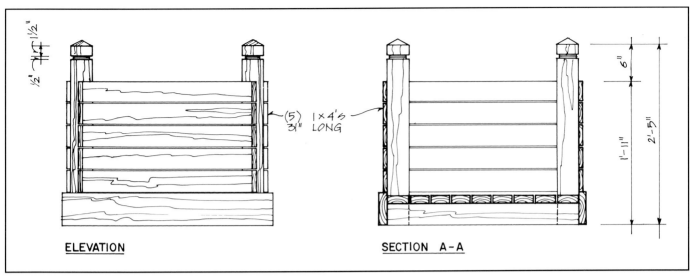

ELEVATION

(5) 1×4's
3" LONG

SECTION A-A

6"

1'-11"

2'-5"

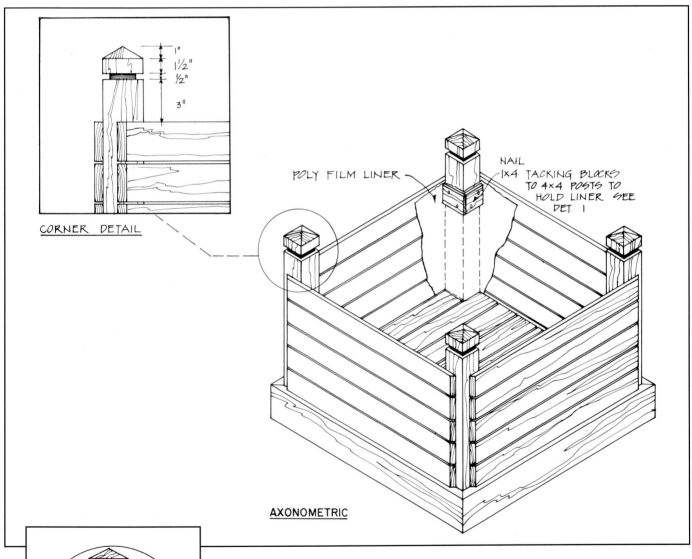

CORNER DETAIL

1"
1½"
½"
3"

POLY FILM LINER

NAIL
1×4 TACKING BLOCKS
TO 4×4 POSTS TO
HOLD LINER SEE
DET. 1

AXONOMETRIC

DET. 1

1"

Courtesy of Southern Pine Council

Picket Fence Planter

Courtesy of Georgia-Pacific

Here's a fanciful, romantic planter for that idyllic, old-fashioned garden. Designed for Georgia-Pacific, it's an easy to assemble piece that will add distinction and beauty to your home.

Materials

Wood
7   1x2s at 8 feet cut to:
>   1 top front and 1 back rail at 2' 9-3/4"
>   2 top side rails at 12"
>   38 pickets at 12-1/4"

1   1x4 at 5 feet cut to:
>   8 post tops and bottoms at 2-1/2" x 2-1/2"
>   2 bottom side rails at 12"

1   2x2 at 5 feet cut to:
>   4 posts at 13.5"

1   2x4x6 cut to:
1 front and 1 back bottom rail at 2' 9-3/4"
>   Exterior cdx plywood for base cut to 2' 9"x12"x1/2"

Other
4 full-round finials, 2" diameter
4 double-threaded finial screws
24 galvanized decking screws, 1-1/2"
1-1/4" galvanized finishing nails
1 tube waterproof construction adhesive

Instructions

1. Cut a 1/2" x 3/8" rabbet the length of the bottom side rails; and a 1/2" x 3/4" rabbet the length of the bottom front and back rails.
2. Glue and screw plywood base into bottom rail rabbets.
3. Cut two 3/4" deep rabbets in each corner post to fit the rails into.
4. Drill weep holes in plywood base.
5. Screw rails together and glue and screw into posts. Glue and nail pickets to rails allowing 3/4" spaces between pickets.
6. Glue and screw post bottoms to posts.
7. Attach finials and post tops to posts with glue and double-threaded finial screws.

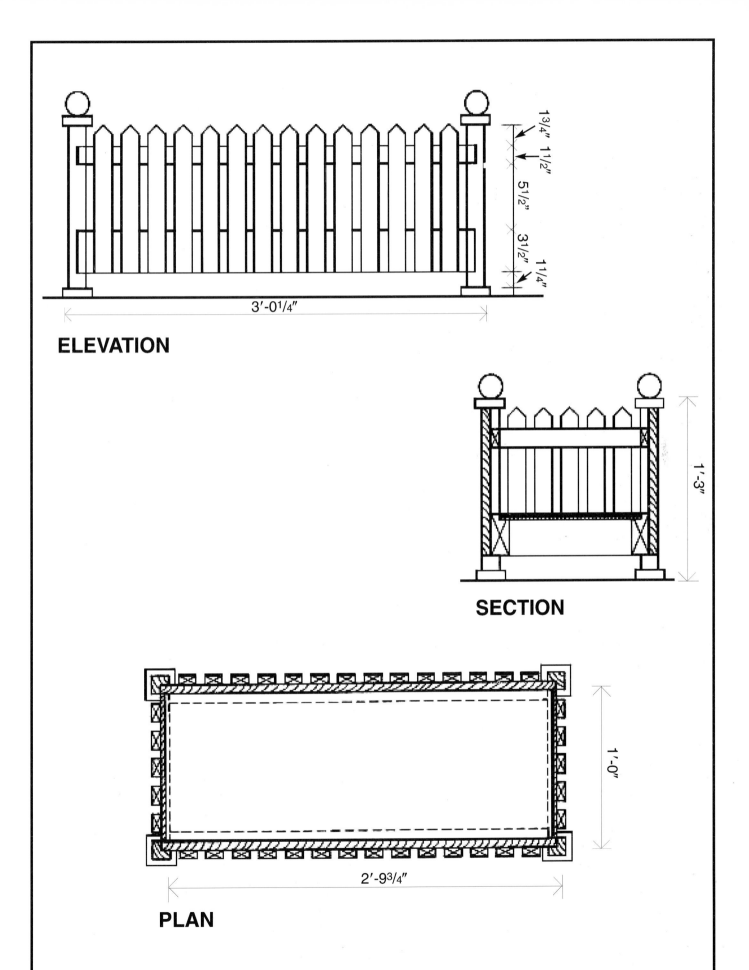

ELEVATION

1¾" 1½"

5½"

3½"

1¼"

3'-0¼"

1'-3"

SECTION

1'-0"

2'-9¾"

PLAN

Decorative Garden Borders

Here are some lovely ideas for your leftovers from Southern Pine Council. Scraps can be cut to form intricate or simple borders. Squares of 1x4 or 2x4 are used for the base, with the decorative border nailed on using decking screws or galvanized nails. To install, dig a 3"-wide trench and backfill, keeping the borders vertical.

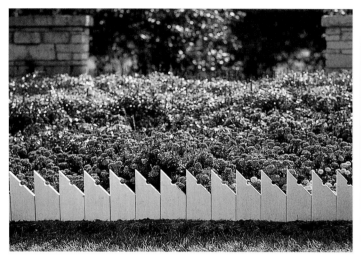 

Courtesy of Southern Pine Council

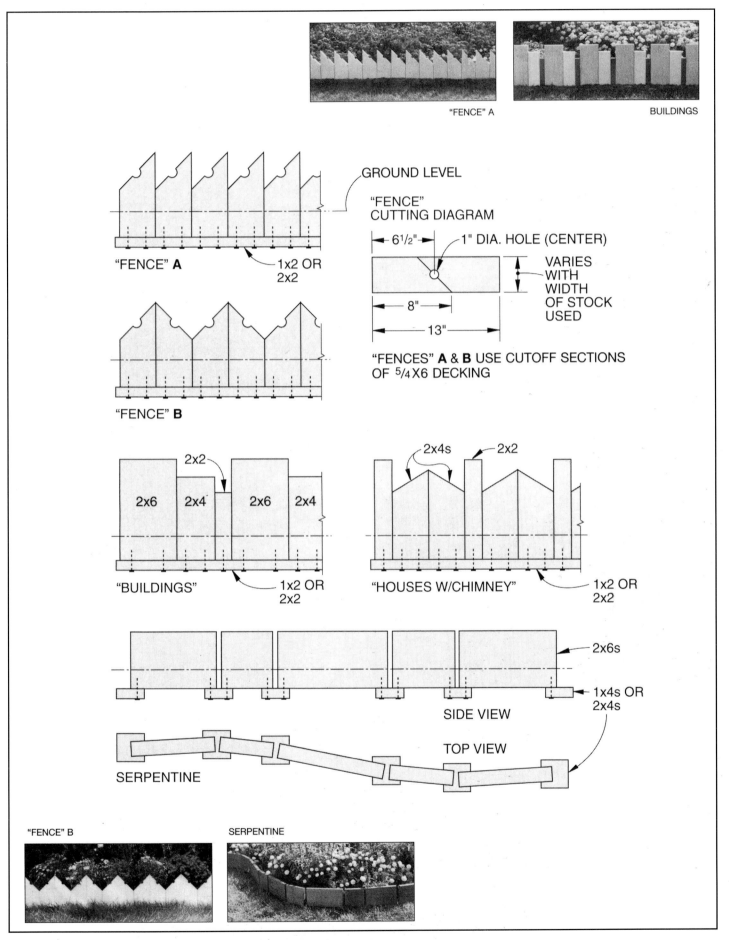

"FENCE" A

BUILDINGS

GROUND LEVEL

"FENCE" CUTTING DIAGRAM

"FENCE" **A**

1x2 OR 2x2

6½" 1" DIA. HOLE (CENTER)

VARIES WITH WIDTH OF STOCK USED

8"

13"

"FENCES" **A** & **B** USE CUTOFF SECTIONS OF ⁵/₄X6 DECKING

"FENCE" **B**

"BUILDINGS"

2x2

2x6   2x4   2x6   2x4

1x2 OR 2x2

"HOUSES W/CHIMNEY"

2x4s   2x2

1x2 OR 2x2

2x6s

1x4s OR 2x4s

SIDE VIEW

TOP VIEW

SERPENTINE

"FENCE" B

SERPENTINE

Courtesy of Southern Pine Council

25

WHERE THE WORK GETS DONE

Work Center

Courtesy of Georgia-Pacific

Maybe you don't have room in the garage or basement, or maybe you'd rather be doing this work outdoors anyway. For starters, Georgia-Pacific suggests this project for an outdoor work station worthy of any handyman or woman.

Materials

Wood
3 sheets of 1/4" x 4' x 8' B-C grade plywood cut to:

>	2 top shelves at 4' x 8"
>	2 inner shelves at 4' x 24"
>	2 sides at 22" wide x 31-1/2" high
>	1 back at 48" wide x 57-1/2" high
>	2 doors at 20-1/8" x 28" high

1 sheet of 23/32" x 4' x 4' B-C grade plywood cut to:
>	48" wide by 28-1/2" for the worktop

10 studs at 2' x 4' x 8' cut to:
>	10 shelf frame fronts and backs at 48"
>	4 shelf frame sides at 5"
>	6 shelf frame sides at 21"
>	1 12" blocking
>	1 48" worktop stiffener
>	2 60" rear legs
>	2 34" front legs

2 1x2x8' boards cut to:
>	4 door frames at 28" tall
>	4 door frames at 17-1/8" wide

Other
2 cabinet knobs
4 cabinet hinges
Wood glue
8d and 16d nails
Drywall screws
Magnetic catch for cabinet doors
Acrylic latex primer and paint or opaque color satin

Instructions

1. Build 2x4 frames for each top and inner shelf. Nail 1/4" plywood flush to all edges.
2. Build 2x4 worktop frame. Nail 3/4" frame plywood flush to rear edge. Leave overhang on front edge.
3. At height indicated on drawing, nail front legs to three lower shelves, then nail on rear legs. Check for square. Attach two upper shelves.
4. Screw plywood sides and back in place leaving 2-1/2" gap from floor.
5. Nail blocking to worktop frame centered between front legs.
6. Nail worktop stiffener over blocking and on top of front legs. Screw down worktop to stiffener.
7. Build cabinet doors by screwing 1/4" plywood over 1x2 frames. Screw cabinet knobs through doors at frames. Attach cabinet doors to front legs using hinges.
8. Sand all rough edges. Prime and paint with primer and acrylic latex paint or opaque color satin.

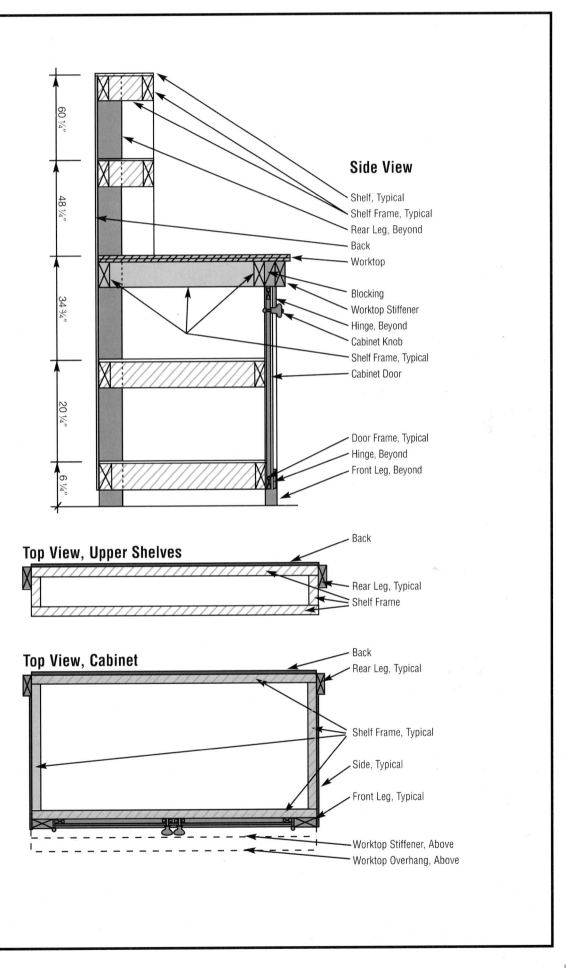

Side View

Shelf, Typical
Shelf Frame, Typical
Rear Leg, Beyond
Back
Worktop
Blocking
Worktop Stiffener
Hinge, Beyond
Cabinet Knob
Shelf Frame, Typical
Cabinet Door

Door Frame, Typical
Hinge, Beyond
Front Leg, Beyond

60 ¼"
48 ¼"
34 ¾"
20 ¼"
6 ¼"

Top View, Upper Shelves

Back
Rear Leg, Typical
Shelf Frame

Top View, Cabinet

Back
Rear Leg, Typical
Shelf Frame, Typical
Side, Typical
Front Leg, Typical
Worktop Stiffener, Above
Worktop Overhang, Above

Potting Shed

Courtesy of Southern Pine Council

Here's an outdoor home for the true gardener from Southern Pine Council. It's a special place to pot plants and store all your tools and supplies. Designed as a free-standing structure, it can be attached to an existing fence, garage, or other building.

Materials

Wood
2   4x4s at 10 feet
1   4x4 at 8 feet
5   2x6s at 6 feet
6   2x4s at 10 feet
1   2x4 at 8 feet
8   2x4s at 6 feet
1   1x8 at 6 feet
14   1x4s at 6 feet

Other
8d, 10d, and 12d hot-dipped galvanized nails
16 1/4" x 3" hot-dipped galvanized lag screws
Two 4x8 sheets of 3/8"-thick pressure-treated plywood siding, T-111 pattern
Water repellent sealer
Concrete blocks or bricks for base

Roof materials
15 pound roofing felt

Asphalt or fiberglass shingles
Roofing nails
Galvanized sheet metal ridge, 6' long
Standard eave drip (galvanized), 6' long
1/2" sheathing plywood, 3'6"x6'

Instructions

1. Cut two 4x4 posts 3' 3-1/2" long. Cut two 4x4 posts 8' 8-1/2" long, making an angle cut on one end to match slope of roof.
2. Using 2x6 material, make the outside frame pieces. Cut four pieces, 2' 2" long; use two 6' lengths for the front pieces.
3. Using 12d nails and construction adhesive, build the main frame assembly. Join 6-foot 2x6s to the front 4x4 posts. Join front and rear posts together with 2x6 outside pieces. Refer to plan. Check to be sure basic frame remains square and level.
4. Using 10d nails and construction adhesive, attach 2x4 frame supports (6) to inside of 4x4 posts. Cut four supports each from a .25 10-foot 2x4. Save the scraps. Note their locations on the plan for proper positioning of shelves.
5. Pre-assemble 2x4 interior frame. Cut six more supports 24-1/2" long from the 10' lengths. Cut two rear posts 8' 8-1/2' long, from two .40 2x4s with an angle cut at the top to match the 4x4 posts. In addition, cut a notch at the top to receive 2x6 cross brace. Make 2x4 front posts by cutting a 6' length in half. Using 10d nails and construction adhesive, build two frames by nailing front and rear 2x4 posts together, each with three supports. Again, note proper positioning to allow for shelves.
6. Cut 3-1/2" shelf cleats from scrap 2x4 material. Nail into place on the inner frame assemblies, on the opposite sides from the shelf supports, using 10d nails. Refer to plan.
7. Cut 2x4 cleats for upper 1x8 shelf. Locate their position on the 2x4 rear posts and nail into place using 10d nails. Also attach two cleats to 4x4 rear posts.
8. Attach 2x4 interior frame by driving 10d nails through the front 2x6 members into the front 2x4 posts. Make sure the frame remains level and square.
9. Cut a 2x6 to 5' 2". Using 10d nails, attach across top of 2x4 rear posts in notches. Toe-nail ends to 4x4 corner posts.
10. From the plywood siding, cut two pieces 48"x57". Nail to the rear of the 4x4 posts and 2x4 frames, using 8d nails and construction adhesive. Position the panels horizontally with the pattern facing the front.
11. Install the main 2x4 shelf. From the 6' lengths, cut six pieces 5'9" long. Attach to 2x4 shelf supports, using 10d nails and construction adhesive. Cut one 2x4 in lengths to fit between rear posts and nail to cleats and supports.
12. Repeat the procedure in Step 10 to install the 1x4 storage shelves.

13. Similarly, attach the 1x8 shelf to 2x4 cleats, using 10d nails. Notch the 1x8 to fit around 2x4 rear posts.
14. Use leftover siding pieces to make side panels. Refer to Step 10. Attach to 4x4 corner posts.
15. Cut four pairs of 2x4 rafters and braces according to the plan. Attach both to frame posts using lag screws and construction adhesive. Join rafter to brace with 2x4 splice plate (made from scrap material) using 10d nails.

16. Attach 1/2" sheathing plywood to rafters using 8d nails.
17. Install roofing felt and shingles. Attach the eave drip across the rafter ends. Attach the metal ridge across the joint of the roof with the rear wall panel. Refer to plan.
18. When complete, coat the unit with water repellent sealer.

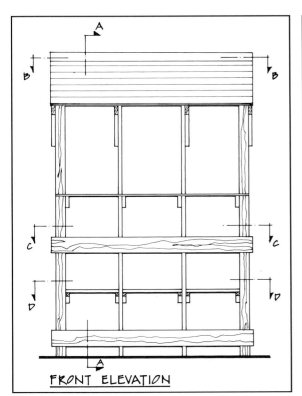

FRONT ELEVATION

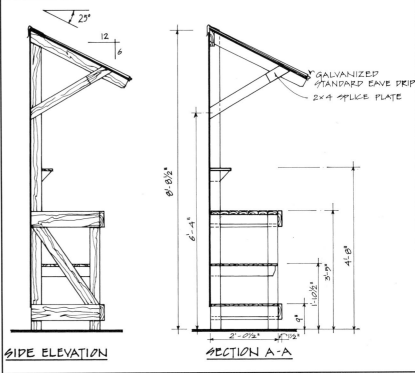

SIDE ELEVATION

SECTION A-A

Courtesy of Southern Pine Council

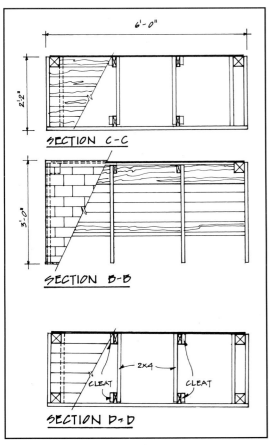

SECTION C-C

SECTION B-B

SECTION D-D

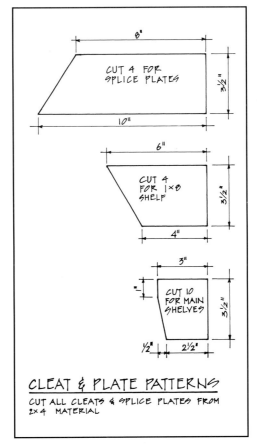

CUT 4 FOR SPLICE PLATES

CUT 4 FOR 1x8 SHELF

CUT 10 FOR MAIN SHELVES

CLEAT & PLATE PATTERNS
CUT ALL CLEATS & SPLICE PLATES FROM 2x4 MATERIAL

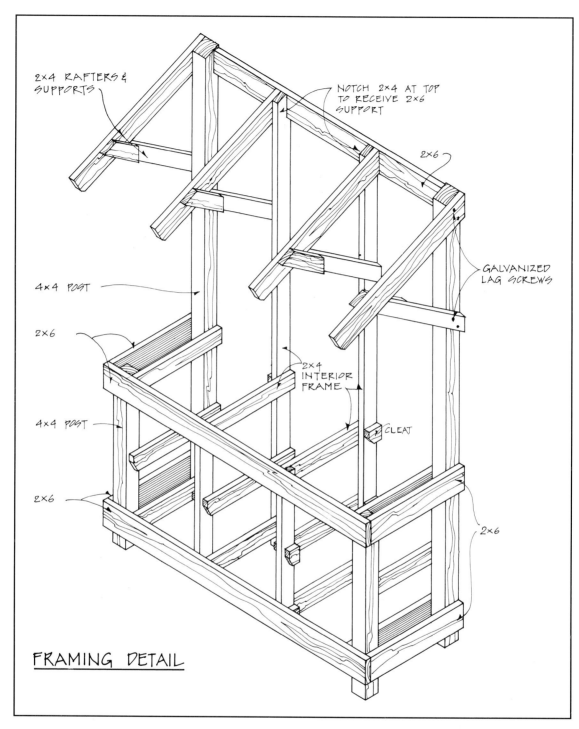

2×4 RAFTERS &
SUPPORTS

NOTCH 2×4 AT TOP
TO RECEIVE 2×6
SUPPORT

2×6

GALVANIZED
LAG SCREWS

4×4 POST

2×6

2×4
INTERIOR
FRAME

4×4 POST

CLEAT

2×6

2×6

FRAMING DETAIL

Courtesy of Southern Pine Council

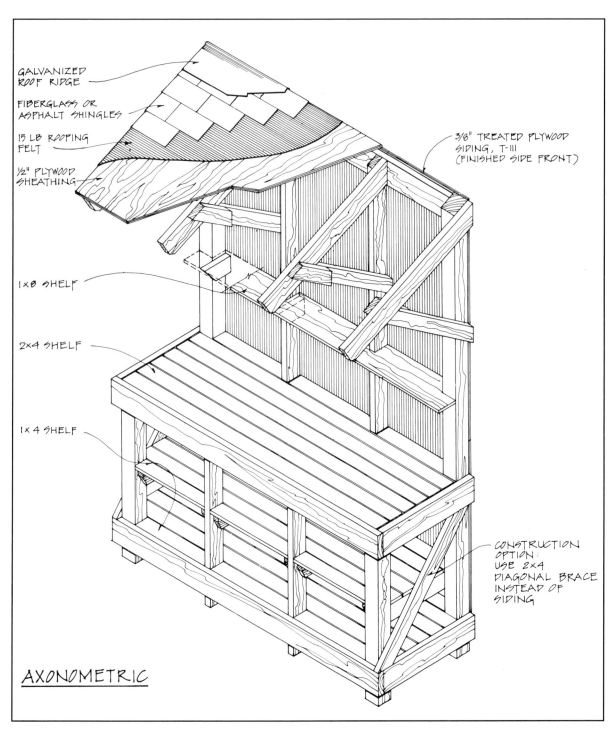

GALVANIZED
ROOF RIDGE

FIBERGLASS OR
ASPHALT SHINGLES

15 LB ROOFING
FELT

1/2" PLYWOOD
SHEATHING

1×8 SHELF

2×4 SHELF

1×4 SHELF

3/8" TREATED PLYWOOD
SIDING, T-111
(FINISHED SIDE FRONT)

CONSTRUCTION
OPTION:
USE 2×4
DIAGONAL BRACE
INSTEAD OF
SIDING

AXONOMETRIC

Courtesy of Southern Pine Council

Garden Shed

Though this is the most complicated project in the book, it will undoubtedly be the most satisfying and, in the long-run, the most used. The Georgia-Pacific Garden Shed was designed to be built by the moderately experienced carpenter. It features platform construction on 4x4 posts sunk in concrete-lined holes similar to standard residential deck construction. Therefore, it can be set on any firm soil, whether sloped or flat, without site preparation.

There are approximately 40 square feet of floor space inside the shed and ample headroom for storage of bicycles, a lawnmower, garden tools, or play equipment. The room is large enough for a six-foot potting bench or workbench. A rear window provides natural light.

The design also includes a hutch on the side big enough for several refuse or recycling bins. Adding insulation, electricity, or running water would expand the use of the room for many purposes.

Materials

Wood
5 12-foot 4x4s for posts
8 8-foot 2x8s for floor and rim joists
3 23/32" thick, 4x8 plywood
8 14-foot 2x4s for sidewall studs
18 10-foot 2x4s for front and rear wall studs
13 16-foot 2x4s for plates, headers, jacks, etc.
3 8-foot 2x4s for door rails and stiles
6 14-foot 2x6s for rafters
1 8-foot 2x8 for ridge beam
5 4x8 sheets of plywood rated sheathing, 15/32", for roof deck
11 4x8 sheets of beaded board panels perforated headboard, 11/32", for interior wall sheathing
4 4x8 sheets of plywood beaded board panels, 11/32", for ceiling

Trim
8 1x6x16 for overdoor, cornerboards and sub-fascia
7 1x4x6 for door and window casing and trim, hutch corner boards, baseboards
2 1-1/4x10x16 for fascia on shed and band
1 1-1/4x6x16 for fascia on recycling hutch
2 1-1/4x6x16 for skirts and band on hutch

Courtesy of Georgia-Pacific

Siding
19/32"x4x8 panels G-P T1-11 plywood siding with 4 inches on center grooves
4 4x8 panels for front and rear facades
7 4x8 panels for side facades and door

Molding and Flashing
Cove molding under fascia edge: 96 linear feet of 3/4" or 1" cove profile
Optional trim on window in door: one casing at 8'
Drip edge on the top of fascia at eave and rake: 5 drip edge at 10'

2x2 flashing overdoor and window: at 10 linear feet
3x3 flashing hutch roof and shed sidewall: at 10 linear feet
Z aluminum flashing: 36 linear feet

Ramp
Top Choice pressure-treated lumber joists: one 2x6x12 (length will vary to accommodate each site)
Decking: three 1-1/4x6x12
Optional footholds: 1x2 cut to 14" long (number varies with length of ramp, spaced every 12")
Concrete and gravel
12 80-pound bags of concrete mix (two bags per hole)
Sufficient gravel to cover ground under shed (optional)

Hardware
3 pairs of strap-style, black door hinges
2 door latches with hasp and lock, black
25 pounds of 16 penny hot-dipped galvanized (HDG) sinkers
10 pounds 1-1/4" HDG roofing nails
10 pounds 8 penny HDG finish nails for trim
10 pounds 8 penny HDG spiral siding nails
5 pounds joist hanger HDG nails

Windows
Rear window: prefabricated 24"x24" wood octagonal venting window with clear glass
Optional: insect screen
Optional window on door: Plexiglass or glass cut to fit

Roof
1 roll G-P 15 pound residential roofing felt
4 bundles G-P Summit® Series shingles
1 bundle G-P hip and ridge shingles in matching color
8 linear feet of roll ridge vent

Optional furnishings
2   1x10x16 pine shelves
2 prefabricated cabinets, 6' long by 36" high
25" deep countertop, cut to fit approximately 6', 3/4" G-P MDF

Trellis
4   12-foot 2x2s for framing
Vinyl coated electrical wire hooks and screw eyes

Paint and Caulk
Approximately two gallons of exterior acrylic latex primer and wall paint
Non-hardening caulk

Instructions

1. **Siting the Shed**. Choose a convenient location, (not necessarily on flat ground). When finished, the bottoms of the floor joists should be at least 6 inches above the ground, high enough that water on the ground cannot reach them. The ramp should be long enough to slope down at a 45-degree angle or less.

2. **Footing and Posts**. Lay out the holes to make certain they are square. Dig the holes for the footings; the depth should be below your local frost line. Make the holes larger than the posts to allow for adjustment (approximately 12" wide). Set four full-length 4 x 4 corner posts in the holes, temporarily bracing them in both directions so they stay plumb. DO NOT pour the concrete. The posts for the hutch should be set after the shed is framed.

3. **Framing**. Hang the rim joists on the posts with joist hangers so the outside faces are flush. Hang the floor joists from the side rim joists using joist hangers at 16" on center or less. Deck the floor with 23/32" plywood.

   Frame the stud walls horizontally on flat ground using standard construction techniques including a sole plate, a single top plate, and studs at 16" on center. Frame the door and window openings leaving the sole plate under the door. Add a nailing surface if you will be adding interior sheathing. Nail the walls in place between the 4x4 posts using 16d sinkers.

   Check the posts to be sure they are plumb and level, and then fill each posthole with two bags of concrete, leaving the top surface sloped to drain water away from the posts. When the concrete has set thoroughly, cut the four posts off flush with the side wall plate. Add a second top plate on top of the side walls extending over the post tops. Add a second top plate on top of the front and rear walls lapping the opposite way over the peaks.

4. **Ridge and Rafters**. Toenail the ridge beam in place between the front and rear walls. Cut the rafter birdsmouths so the level (seat) cuts are 3-1/2" long where they sit on the top plate. The plumb cuts are perpendicular to the seat cuts. Let the rafter tails run wild (long) to be trimmed later. Lay out the rafter spacing on the ridge using five rafters evenly spaced on each side.

5. **Siding**. Wrap the entire structure with tarpaper or building wrap. Nail band to rim joists, and skirt above band to stud walls. Before cutting the siding, lay out the cutting lines on the plywood following the enclosed patterns so that the grooves do not fall on a cornerboard and so the center of the facade is centered between two grooves. Slip the flashing for the shed roof and overdoor trim under the siding before nailing it to the studs, and Z-flashing under the bottom of the siding and over the skirts.

6. **Roof**. To calculate the rafter tail length mock-up the fascias on the front facade following the dotted lines in the detail drawing provided. Cut the rafter tails so that the fascias will neatly wrap around the building corners. The grooves in the siding meet the sub-fascia allowing the roof to vent. Sheath the roof with 15/32" plywood. Apply the roof felt

and shingles following manufacturer's instructions. Cover the ridge with ridge vent.

7. **Door and Window.** Cut the door out of siding and apply 2x4s flat for stiffening and add a diagonal brace from top hinge down to the lower corner on the swinging side.

Optional: Add a small window made of Plexiglass, window glass or insect screen trimmed with small-dimensioned window stop and use small strips of lattice for decorative muntins. Hang the door in the cased opening using decorative strap hinges mounted on pads so they lay flat with the door trim. Leave the sole plate under the door as a door stop. Install window in rear wall.

8. **Trim.** Apply the sub-fascia and fascia on top of the siding. Apply cove molding to trim the bottom and top edges. Add a drip edge at the top of the fascias under the roof deck. Next cut the cornerboards to fit between the skirts and fascias. Add the cornerboards to the front and rear facades, then butt the side cornerboards to them so the caulk joint does not show from the main facades. Add the door and window casing and the overdoor and overwindow trim. Add the drip edge to the side and top edges of the overdoor and overwindow trim.

9. **Ramp.** Make the ramp from 2x6 pressure treated joists with 5/4 x 6 decking nailed on top. Make it long enough that it slopes down at less than a 45-degree angle. Optional: If your ramp is long or steep apply footholds at 12-inch intervals or at whatever distance is comfortable for your stride and the angle you have chosen; be sure you can get your lawnmower or other equipment easily around the footholds.

If you are using the shed for bicycles or a wheelbarrow, two sets of footholds with a space in between for the wheel would be convenient.

10. **Interior.** Finish the interior to suit your planned use of the shed. Insulation and Ply-Bead would make it cozy and finished. G-P perforated hardboard would make it functional for tool storage. Shelves and cabinets would be useful for a potting shed if there is water available nearby. A serious gardener may want a large sink. A workbench and power source would make a functional workshop.

11. **Trellis.** Lay out the 2 x 2 lattice work as shown in the elevation drawing. Where two boards overlap mark the overlaps on both boards with a pencil line. Cut and chisel out half the depth of the wood between the pencil lines to make half-lap joints and reassemble the layout with the boards lapped together. Use vinyl-coated electrical wire to form support for your plants by weaving it between the boards. When you are satisfied with the pattern, screw joints together. Hang the trellis from screw eyes with hooks to make it easy to demount for fall cleanup and to repaint the wall behind it without uprooting your plantings.

12. **Paint.** Caulk joints carefully except where the siding meets the soffit. Paint or opaque stain the shed to suit your style preference.

13. **Recycling Hutch.** The hutch is built using the same construction techniques and sequence as the shed except that a ledger board attaches it to the shed much as a deck is attached to a house. Cut the remaining 8-foot 4 x 4 posts in half to make the two corner posts. Add flashing where the roof meets the shed siding.

FRONT VIEW

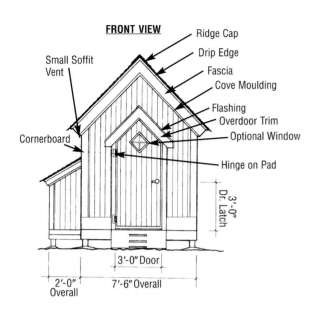

- Ridge Cap
- Drip Edge
- Fascia
- Cove Moulding
- Small Soffit Vent
- Flashing
- Overdoor Trim
- Optional Window
- Cornerboard
- Hinge on Pad
- Dr. Latch
- 3'-0"
- 3'-0" Door
- 2'-0" Overall
- 7'-6" Overall

EAVE DETAIL

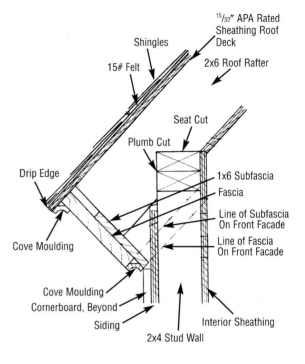

- Shingles
- 15# Felt
- $^{15}/_{32}$" APA Rated Sheathing Roof Deck
- 2x6 Roof Rafter
- Seat Cut
- Plumb Cut
- 1x6 Subfascia
- Fascia
- Line of Subfascia On Front Facade
- Line of Fascia On Front Facade
- Drip Edge
- Cove Moulding
- Cove Moulding
- Cornerboard, Beyond
- Siding
- 2x4 Stud Wall
- Interior Sheathing

SIDE 1

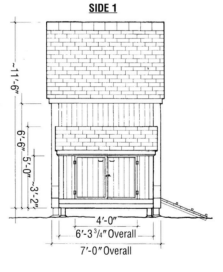

- ~11'-6"
- 6'-6"
- 5'-0"
- ~3'-2"
- 4'-0"
- 6'-3 ¾" Overall
- 7'-0" Overall

SIDE 2

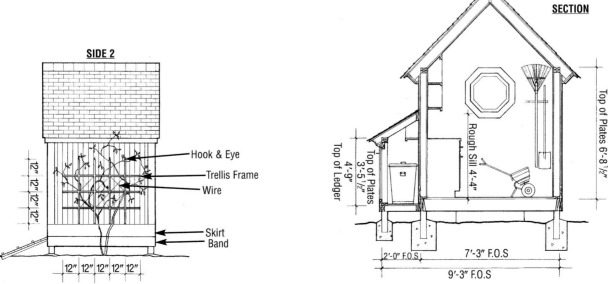

- Hook & Eye
- Trellis Frame
- Wire
- Skirt Band
- 12" 12" 12" 12"
- 12" 12" 12" 12" 12"

SECTION

- Top of Plates 6'-8½"
- Rough Sill 4'-4"
- Top of Plates 3'-5½"
- Top of Ledger
- 4'-9"
- 2'-0" F.O.S
- 7'-3" F.O.S
- 9'-3" F.O.S

Courtesy of Georgia-Pacific

35

SECTION

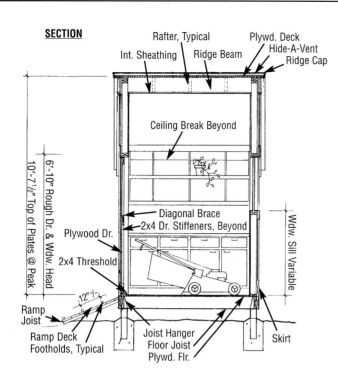

Rafter, Typical
Plywd. Deck
Hide-A-Vent
Ridge Cap
Int. Sheathing
Ridge Beam

Ceiling Break Beyond

10'-7 1/2" Top of Plates @ Peak
6'-10" Rough Dr. & Wdw. Head

Diagonal Brace
2x4 Dr. Stiffeners, Beyond
Plywood Dr.

2x4 Threshold

Wdw. Sill Variable

12"±

Ramp Joist

Ramp Deck
Footholds, Typical

Joist Hanger
Floor Joist
Plywd. Flr.

Skirt

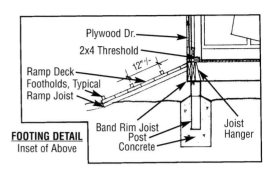

Plywood Dr.

2x4 Threshold

Ramp Deck
Footholds, Typical
Ramp Joist

12"±

Band Rim Joist
Post
Concrete

Joist Hanger

FOOTING DETAIL
Inset of Above

SIDE CUTTING PATTERNS

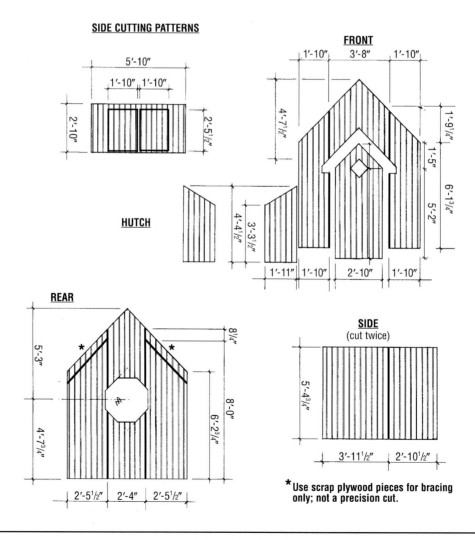

5'-10"

1'-10"   1'-10"

2'-10"

2'-5 1/2"

HUTCH

4'-4 1/2"

3'-3 1/2"

FRONT

1'-10"   3'-8"   1'-10"

4'-7 1/2"

1'-9 1/4"

1'-5"

6'-1 3/4"

5'-2"

1'-11"   1'-10"   2'-10"   1'-10"

REAR

5'-3"

4'-7 3/4"

8 1/4"

8'-0"

6'-2 3/4"

4"

2'-5 1/2"   2'-4"   2'-5 1/2"

SIDE
(cut twice)

5'-4 3/4"

3'-11 1/2"   2'-10 1/2"

*Use scrap plywood pieces for bracing only; not a precision cut.

Courtesy of Georgia-Pacific

36

Storage Shed

Enjoying your backyard can be relaxing, but it can also get crowded. There's lawn furniture, gardening tools and supplies, maybe pool equipment. And don't forget the bicycles, tools, and other odds and ends that just can't find a parking place in the garage or basement. An outdoor storage facility is the answer to your bulky storage problems.

This plan, developed for the Southern Pine Council, is adaptable to meet your storage needs. Three flooring options are specified, and an optional ramp can be built to help get a wheelbarrow or riding mower in or out more easily. Inside, the 2x4 stud wall will simplify the installation of shelves or hardware from which to hang tools. The pressure treated exterior siding can be painted, stained, or left to weather naturally to a silver-gray color.

The plan calls for a very heavy-duty 2x6 floor. It is designed to support heavy lawn equipment and large containers. If your storage needs are less demanding, consider a floor of 3/4" exterior grade plywood (3 4x8 sheets) or a floor of pressure-treated 1x6 boards (18 10-foot lengths).

Materials

Wood

2 4x6s at 10'
2 2x8s at 10'
11 2x8s at 8'
18 2x6s at 10'
49 2x4s at 8'
6 2x4s at 10'
7 2x6s at 12'
1 1x6 at 10'
4 1x8s at 10'
2 1x4s at 8'
8 1x2s at 8'
11 4x8s plywood siding sheets, pattern TJ-111, 1/2" thick

Other

6d, 8d, 10d, 12d hot-dipped galvanized nails
3 pair galvanized butt hinges, Stanley F1798P or similar
Water repellent sealer
Construction adhesive for pressure treated wood
Door handles and closure hardware (lock and hasp)

Courtesy of Southern Pine Council

Roofing Materials (to cover 120 square feet)

15 pound roofing felt
5 4x8 sheets of sheathing plywood, 1/2" thick
Galvanized standard eave drips: 2-10', 4-6'
Roofing nails
Fiberglass or asphalt shingles

Instructions

1. Determine the exact location of your shed. Position 4x6 skids at ground level, parallel to the front and rear of the shed. Use stakes, line, and level to aid placement of skids.
2. Cut the two 10-foot 2x8s to 9' 11" and four of the 8-foot 2x8s to 7' 8" long. Build the 2x8 base frame with these members, using 10d nails and construction adhesive. Use a double 2x8 on each side. Refer to plan and detail section "D."
3. Toe-nail base frame to 4x6 skids using 12d nails and construction adhesive. Check to be sure base is level and square.
4. Install seven 2x8 floor joists (cut to 7' 8") 16 inches on center, according to plan. Attach to base frame using 10d nails (end nailing), 12d nails (toe-nail) and construction adhesive. Check each joist/frame joint for square.
5. Attach a 10' 2x4 (trimmed to 9' 11") to top front and rear edge of base frame; use 10d nails. This becomes a plate for 2x4 stud wall.
6. Install 2x6 floor. Trim the 18 10-foot 2x6s to 9' 11". Attach to base frame and floor joists using 10d nails and construction adhesive.
7. Fabricate the rear 2x4 stud wall using 7' 7-1/2" lengths. Use a double 2x4 on each end, with studs 16" on center, plus an extra stud at the center. Nail studs to 9' 11" 2x4 top and bottom members using 10d nails. Refer to plan and detail section "C." Attach finished wall frame to 2x4 plate with 10d nails and construction adhesive.
8. Fabricate the two side wall 2x4 frames; using 7' 7-1/2" lengths 16" on center. Start at the center of the 7' 4" wall section and space studs as shown on the plan. Nail studs to 2x4 top and bottom members using 10d nails. Attach finished wall frame to ends of floor boards using 10d nails and construction adhesive.
9. Fabricate front wall 2x4 framing using 7' 7-1/2" lengths. End sections are double-end 2x4s with a center stud nailed to common 2x4s top and bottom. Finished wall frame is 2' 10-3/4" wide. Attach to 2x4 plate using 10d nails and construction adhesive. At the doors, the inside 2x4s are cut 6' 9" from top of base frame to support double 2x6

header (4' 3" long) over door opening. Use 10d nails for all framing assembly. Refer to Sections A&B for details.

10. Connect wall frame sections with 2x4 top plates. Use 7' 11" lengths at the sides and 9' 4" lengths front and rear: attach with 10d nails. Front and rear top plates become rafter supports. Wall framing is complete; check for square.

11. Cut 2x6 rafters from 12-foot lengths. Refer to plan for roof slope and notch detail.

12. Cut two 2x4 supports for the 1x6 ridge board; make each support 2' 9" long. Notch one end to receive 2x6 end rafters. Toe-nail into place at center of side walls using 12d nails. Attach 1x6 ridge board using 8d nails and construction adhesive. Ridge board should extend one inch above 2x4 center support.

13. Install roof rafters 2' 0" on center. Nail to ridge board using 10d nails; toe-nail to rafter support using 12d nails. Framing is complete.

14. Enclose wall framing with treated plywood siding panels. Attach to studs using 6d nails and construction adhesive.

15. Attach 1x8 fascia to ends of rafters using 6d nails and construction adhesive.

16. Cover roof framing with 1/2" sheathing plywood; use 6d nails and construction adhesive. Add a layer of roofing felt. Attach galvanized eave drips to roof edges with roofing nails. Install shingles with roofing nails.

17. Complete trim work. Install corner trim to cover plywood siding joints, using 1x2 material. Add 1x4 trim to cover siding panel joint on side walls; trim 8' lengths to fit between corner trim. Cut 1x8 material for exterior gable trim, matching the profile of the rafters. Attach flush with edges of roofing and 1x8 fascia. Install all trim using 8d nails and construction adhesive.

18. Build the two doors. Cut two panels of treated siding 2' 0" wide by 6' 8" high. Attach the 2x4 frame as shown in the plan. Hinge side of 2x4 frame flush with edge of panel. Recess top and door handle side of frame 1 inch from edge of siding panel. Recess bottom member of doorframe 2 inches to clear floorboards when door is closed.

Add diagonal 2x4 brace. Build frame using 10d nails and construction adhesive. Attach siding to frame using 6d nails and construction adhesive. Attach siding to frame using 6d nails and construction adhesive. Hang doors using the galvanized butt hinges and screws. Add your choice of door handles, plus some kind of lock and hasp for security, if desired.

19. Refer to the plan if you want to build the optional 3'x4' ramp to help you move heavy tools and equipment in or out more easily. Cut a 2x8 diagonally for the sides, add a 4' length to the ends, plus a 2x6 and 2x4 brace inside. Use 10d nails and construction adhesive to build this simple frame. Attach a treated siding plywood panel to the top using 6d nails and construction adhesive.

20. Construction is complete. Apply a coat of water repellent sealer to the floor and all exterior wood surfaces.

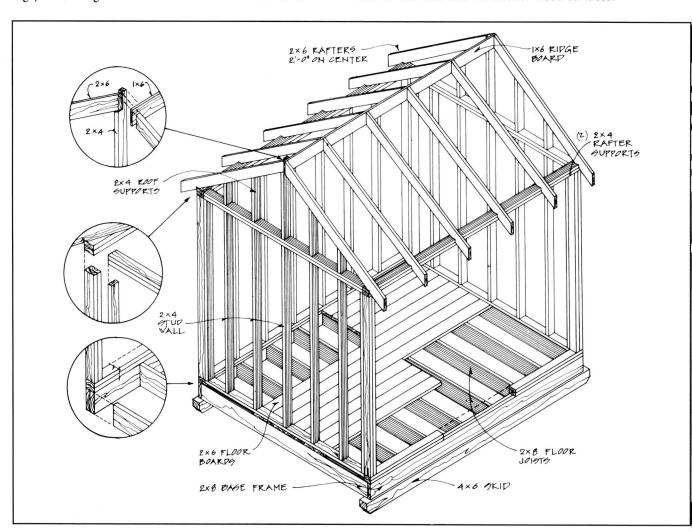

Courtesy of Southern Pine Council

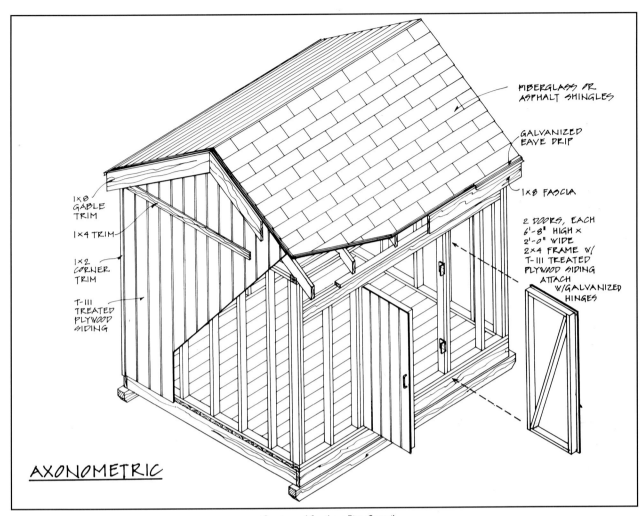

FIBERGLASS OR ASPHALT SHINGLES

GALVANIZED EAVE DRIP

1×8 FASCIA

2 DOORS, EACH 6'-8" HIGH × 2'-0" WIDE 2×4 FRAME W/ T-III TREATED PLYWOOD SIDING ATTACH W/GALVANIZED HINGES

1×8 GABLE TRIM

1×4 TRIM

1×2 CORNER TRIM

T-III TREATED PLYWOOD SIDING

AXONOMETRIC

Courtesy of Southern Pine Council

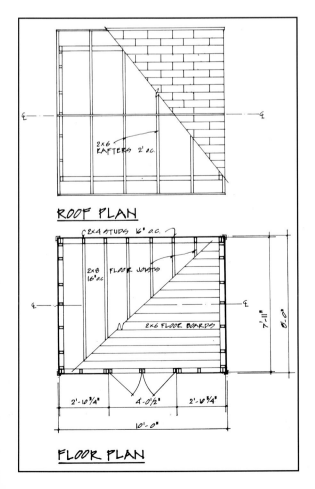

2×6 RAFTERS 2' O.C.

ROOF PLAN

2×4 STUDS 16' O.C.

2×8 FLOOR JOISTS 16' O.C.

2×6 FLOOR BOARDS

7'-11"

8'-0"

2'-10¾"   4'-0½"   2'-10¾"

10'-0"

FLOOR PLAN

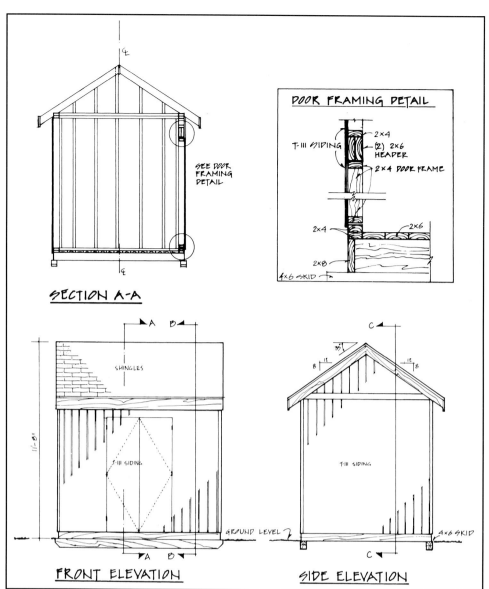

SECTION A-A

DOOR FRAMING DETAIL

T-III SIDING
2×4
(2) 2×6 HEADER
2×4 DOOR FRAME
2×4
2×6
2×8
4×6 SKID

SEE DOOR FRAMING DETAIL

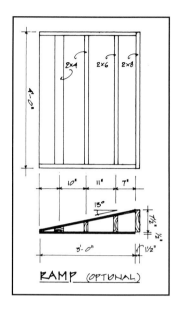

RAMP (OPTIONAL)

2×4   2×6   2×8

4'-0"

10"   11"   7"

13°

3'-0"

1½"

SHINGLES

T-III SIDING

11'-6"

FRONT ELEVATION

3°

8   12   12   8

T-III SIDING

GROUND LEVEL

4×6 SKID

SIDE ELEVATION

Courtesy of Southern Pine Council

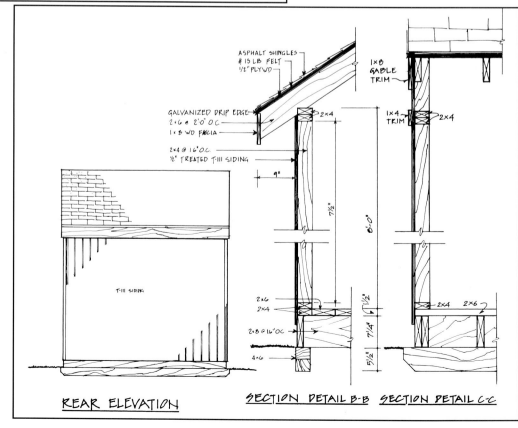

T-III SIDING

REAR ELEVATION

ASPHALT SHINGLES
15 LB FELT
½" PLYWD

GALVANIZED DRIP EDGE
2×6 @ 2'-0" O.C.
1×8 WD FASCIA

2×4 @ 16" O.C.
½" TREATED T-III SIDING

9"

7½"

6'-0"

2×6
2×4

2×8 @ 16" O.C.

4×6

1×8 GABLE TRIM

1×4 TRIM

2×4

2×4   2×6

1½"
7¼"
5½"

SECTION DETAIL B-B   SECTION DETAIL C-C

40

Trash Can and Firewood Storage Unit

Courtesy of Southern Pine Council

Taking out the trash and chopping firewood can be two chores no one really enjoys. And most people don't want the sight of trash cans and firewood to be part of their backyard landscape. To solve both concerns, Glenn C. Higgins, AIA, designed this handy storage unit for the Southern Pine Council. The unit was designed to hold two 20-32 gallon containers, but the dimensions can easily be adjusted to fit a convenient location or to handle larger containers.

Materials

Wood
1 2x4 at 8'
6 2x4s at 12'
2 2x4s at 10'
1 2x4 at 12'
1 2x2 at 6'
3 4x8s sheets of plywood siding, pattern T-111, 1/2" thick
Other
6d, 10d hot-dipped galvanized nails
Two pair 3" galvanized butt hinges with screws
Door handles and closure hardware (lock & hasp)
Construction adhesive for pressure treated wood
Water repellent sealer
Roofing materials
1 sheet 4x8 sheathing plywood, 1/2" thick
Roofing felt
Asphalt or fiberglass shingles

Roofing nails
Galvanized roof ridge, 6' long

Instructions

1. Pre-cut many of the 2x4 pieces you will need as follows:
    From the 8–foot 2x4 cut three bottom frame supports, each 2' 2-1/2" long.
    From one of the 12-foot 2x4s cut the remaining bottom frame members; cut two pieces 3' 10-1/2" long and two pieces 1' 9" long.
    From another 12-foot 2x4 cut the two rear corner posts each 4' 1" long, plus one front corner post 3' 3" long. Refer to plan for roof slope; cut 2x4 tops to match.
    From another 12-foot 2x4 cut front and rear center supports 3' 8" and 2' 11" long respectively. Notch them at the top to receive 2x4 brace. Refer to plan. Also, cut the other front corner post 3' 3" long.
    From a 12-foot 2x4 cut the front and rear top supports 5' 9" long.
    From each of the two 10-foot 2x4s cut two rafters 3' 4" long and one end brace 2' 2-1/2" long. Refer to plan for roof slope and notching required to make rafters.
2. Build the 2x4 frame according to the plan. Using 10d nails and construction adhesive, assemble bottom frame, add corner and center posts. Check to be sure frame remains level and square.
3. Locate position of end braces and attach to corner posts using 10d nails. Rear end of brace should be flush with rear corner posts. Refer to plan.
4. Install 2x4 top supports (front and rear), fitting them to the notched center posts. Nail to center posts. Toe-nail to corner posts. End-nail front support to braces. Use 10d nails and construction adhesive. Check again for level and square.
5. At rear corner posts, use scrap 2x4 material to add blocking between end braces and rear top support. Attach to corner posts using 10d nails.
6. Toe-nail rafters into place, evenly spacing them across span of top supports. Use 10d nails and construction adhesive. End rafters can also be attached to corner posts. Refer to plan.
7. Cut a panel of the treated plywood siding to 4' by 6'. Attach to rear corner and center posts using 6d nails and construction adhesive. Tops of plywood panel and posts should be flush.
8. Cut six floor deck boards from the three remaining 12-foot 2x4s. Notch front and rear members (as required) to fit around center posts. Position floor deck members 1" apart; refer to plan. Recess front member 1/2" for door. Attach floor deck to bottom framing using 10d nails and construction adhesive.

41

9. Cut treated siding panels to fit sides. Position them between corner posts and flush with bottom frame and end rafter. Attach to frame and rafter using 6d nails and construction adhesive.

10. Cut a square 2' by 4' panel from the siding to make a divider panel. Attach to center posts using 6d nails and construction adhesive.

11. Build the two doors. Cut two plywood panels, each measuring 1' 10-3/4" wide by 2' 3" high. Using 6d nails and construction adhesive, attach 2x2 frame to inside of panel. Frame is flush with plywood edges on three sides; allow siding to extend 2 inches at bottom to clear floor deck.

12. Attach door to posts with galvanized butt hinges. Door siding panel and frame of unit should be flush when doors are closed. Add your choice of door handles and closure hardware. Refer to details on plan. Fabricate a door stop using scrap plywood siding; attach to front top support with 6d nails and construction adhesive.

13. Install the roof. Attach half-inch sheathing plywood to rafters using 6d nails and construction adhesive. This panel should cover the area outlined by the corner posts and rafters. Cover with roofing felt, then your choice of shingles; use roofing nails. Attach galvanized roof ridge to the rear corner and center posts using 6d nails.

14. Construction is complete. Apply a coat of water repellent sealer to all exterior surfaces and to the floor deck.

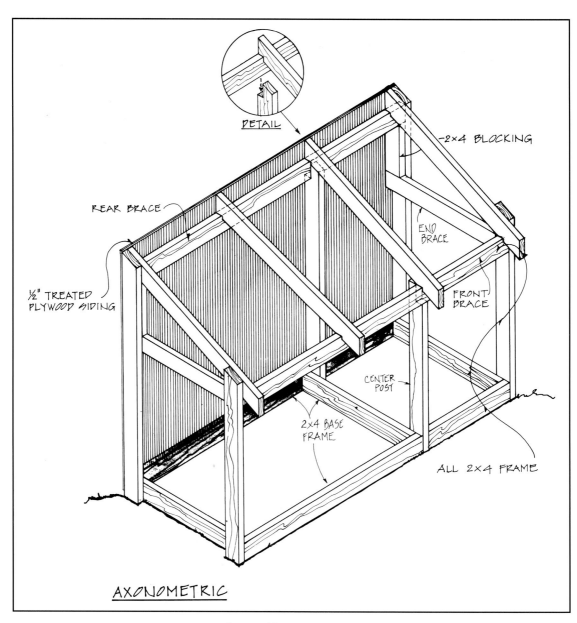

DETAIL

AXONOMETRIC

REAR BRACE

2×4 BLOCKING

END BRACE

FRONT BRACE

½" TREATED PLYWOOD SIDING

CENTER POST

2×4 BASE FRAME

ALL 2×4 FRAME

Courtesy of Southern Pine Council

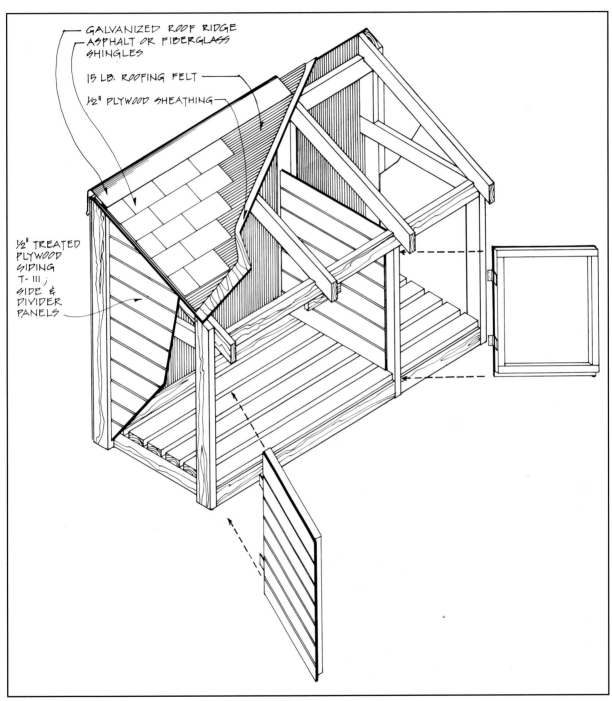

GALVANIZED ROOF RIDGE
ASPHALT OR FIBERGLASS
SHINGLES

15 LB. ROOFING FELT

½" PLYWOOD SHEATHING

½" TREATED
PLYWOOD
SIDING
T-III ;
SIDE &
DIVIDER
PANELS

Courtesy of Southern Pine Council

43

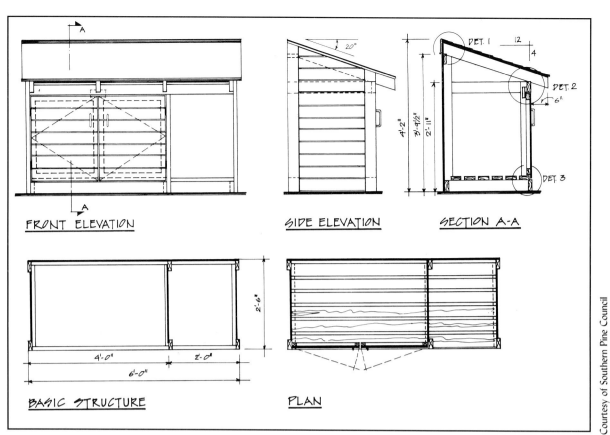

FRONT ELEVATION

SIDE ELEVATION

SECTION A-A

20°

4'-2"
3'-4½"
2'-11"

DET. 1

12
4

DET. 2
6"

DET. 3

BASIC STRUCTURE

4'-0"   2'-0"
6'-0"

2'-6"

PLAN

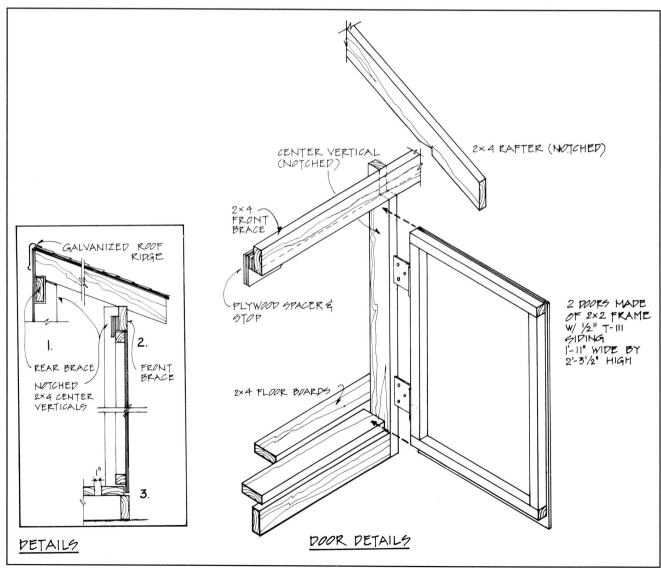

GALVANIZED ROOF RIDGE

1.

2.

3.

REAR BRACE

FRONT BRACE

NOTCHED 2×4 CENTER VERTICALS

DETAILS

CENTER VERTICAL (NOTCHED)

2×4 RAFTER (NOTCHED)

2×4 FRONT BRACE

PLYWOOD SPACER & STOP

2×4 FLOOR BOARDS

2 DOORS MADE OF 2×2 FRAME W/ ½" T-111 SIDING 1'-11" WIDE BY 2'-3½" HIGH

DOOR DETAILS

PLACES TO SIT A SPELL

Slatted-seat Bench

Courtesy of Southern Pine Council

Outdoor furniture must be comfortable and durable. This plan, designed and drawn by Riitta Vepsäläinen for the Southern Pine Council, will take you step-by-step through the construction of your new bench. The low-profile design is both contemporary and functional. When you complete it, you can look forward to years of relaxing comfort. While you're at it, build a matching pair for some attractive corner seating on your deck or patio.

Materials

Wood
1   2x12 at 10'
1   2x12 at 8'
11 2x4 at 6'

Other
8-5/16"x3" and 12-5/16"x4" galvanized lag screws
10d and 12d hot-dipped galvanized nails.
Enough neoprene (hard, compressed rubber) to make 45 3-1/2" squares 1/4" thick
Construction adhesive for pressure treated lumber
Water repellent sealer

Instructions

1. Cut all the pieces need to assemble your bench as follows:
   From the 10-foot 2x12 cut one piece 5' 8" long; six pieces 6-1/4" long for center supports
   From the 8-foot 2x12 cut one piece 5' 8" long; four pieces 6-1/4" long to make end supports
   From the 6-foot 2x4 cut three pieces 11-1/4" long; two pieces 17-1/4" long
   Trim the remaining ten 2x4s to 5' 8" in length

2. Prefabricate two vertical support assemblies. Mark the locations of all end and center supports on the 5' 8"-long 2x12s.

3. To aid the lag screw installation, tack each support into place using a 10d nail.

4. Drill 1/4" holes through the 2x12 into the end and center supports to receive lag screws.

5. Use a hex or socket wrench to install 2-3" lag screws into each end support and 2-4" lag screws into each center support.

6. Locate position of three 2x4 spacers, 11-1/4" long, to fit between vertical support assemblies. Nail all three spacers to one assembly using 10d nails. (Note: Spacers can be extended 24" into the ground and set in concrete to provide permanent positioning of bench. See plan.)

7. Line up the two vertical support assemblies. Fasten together using 12d nails and construction adhesive.

8. Build frame of seating deck, nailing two 2x4s, each 17-1/4" long, to ends of two 2x4s, each 5' 8" long. Use 10d nails and construction adhesive. Pre-drill holes or blunt nail points to avoid splitting. Check to be sure completed frame is square.

9. Arrange eight 2x4s vertically within the frame using quarter-inch neoprene spacers between them. Secure spacers (in line with center and end supports) with construction adhesive. Secure all 2x4s in place by nailing through the two end 2x4s of the frame. Use 10d nails and construction adhesive at these joints, also. Check to be sure seating deck remains square.

10. Run a bead of construction adhesive across the top edge of all 2x12 vertical, end, and center supports. Align seating deck with support assembly as shown in the plan. Only the two 2x4 frame ends should overhang.

11. Using 12d nails, toe-nail seating deck to support assembly. Use one nail through the side of the seating deck into each center support.

12. Coat with water repellent sealer.

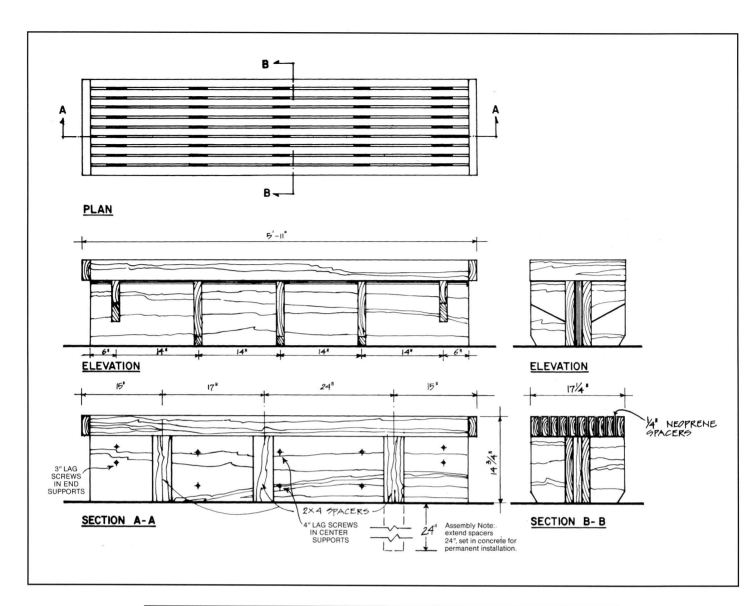

PLAN

5'-11"

ELEVATION

6" · 14" · 14" · 14" · 14" · 6"

ELEVATION

15' · 17" · 24" · 15"

3" LAG SCREWS IN END SUPPORTS

14 3/4"

SECTION A-A

2×4 SPACERS

4" LAG SCREWS IN CENTER SUPPORTS

24"

Assembly Note:. extend spacers 24", set in concrete for permanent installation.

17 1/4"

1/4" NEOPRENE SPACERS

SECTION B-B

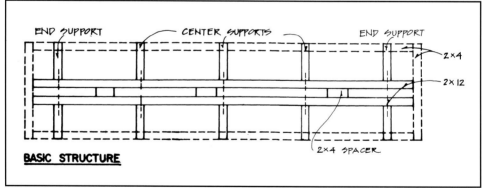

END SUPPORT   CENTER SUPPORTS   END SUPPORT

2×4

2×12

2×4 SPACER

BASIC STRUCTURE

Courtesy of Southern Pine Council

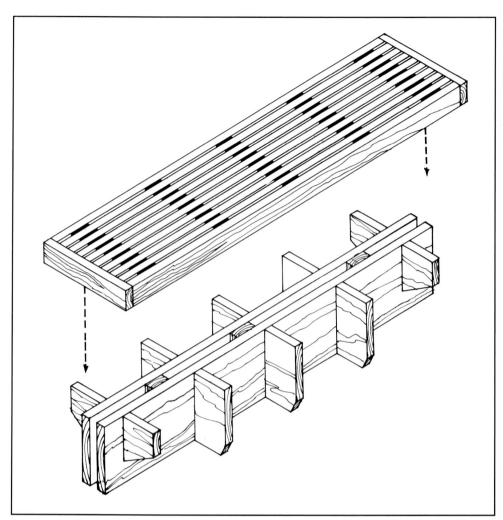

Courtesy of Southern Pine Council

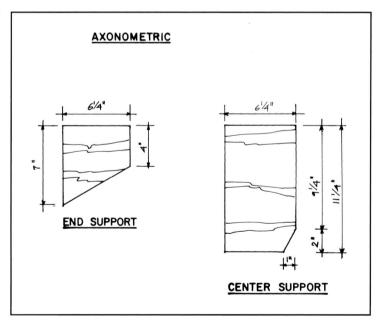

AXONOMETRIC

6¼"

4"

7"

END SUPPORT

6¼"

9¼"

11¼"

2"

1"

CENTER SUPPORT

Planter Bench

Courtesy of Southern Pine Council

Outdoor accents to your deck or patio can be both comfortable and useful. A planter bench can function much like the sofa and end table do indoors. Here's a simple yet elegant accent for your lawn, designed by Raul Quintana for the Southern Pine Council. This plan will guide you through the construction process, step by step. When it's completed, add your choice of plants, have a seat, and enjoy your new addition to better outdoor living.

Materials

Wood
1 2x12 at 12'
4 2x4 at 12'
1 2x4 at 8'
3 2x4 at 10'
1 1x6 at 6'

Other
6d, 8d, 10d hot-dipped galvanized nails
Construction adhesive for pressure treated lumber.
Two heavy-duty plastic garbage bags, 20 or 30-gallon size, for planter liner
Water repellent sealer

Instructions

1. Cut all the pieces needed to assemble your planter bench as follows:

    From the 12-foot 2x12 cut two pieces 4' 4" long; three pieces 12-1/4" long

    From a 12-foot 2x4 cut four pieces 14-1/4" long, two pieces 12-3/4" long, three pieces 16-3/4" long

    From the 8-foot 2x4 cut five pieces 18-1/4" long

    From a 10-foot 2x4 cut one piece 4' 10" long; two pieces 21-1/4" long

    From two 10-foot 2x4s cut four pieces 4' 7" long

    From one 12-foot 2x4 cut one piece 4' 8-1/2" long; four pieces 21-1/4" long

    From a 12-foot 2x4 cut one piece 3' 3-1/2" long; four pieces 21-1/4"

    From a 12-foot 2x4 cut one piece 4' 7" long; four pieces 21-1/4" long

    From the 6-foot 1x6 cut three pieces 19-3/4" long
    Save the scraps.

2. Using 10d nails and construction adhesive, assemble bench frame with 2x12 pieces. Join one 12-1/4" piece flush with each end of the 4' 4" members. Attach 12-1/4" center support; refer to plan. Check to be sure frame is square.

3. Assemble bench seating deck. Attach four 2x4 cross members 1' 6-1/4" long to 2x2 frame using 8d nails and construction adhesive. Note on the plan how the two end cross members overhang 1-1/2"; the other two cross members are evenly spaced between them.

4. Evenly space the five 2x4 decking members, each 4' 7" long, and attach to cross members using construction adhesive and 10d nails. Ends of the decking should be flush with the two end cross members. Refer to plan.

5. Using 8d nails and construction adhesive, attach the two 2x4 edge members, 1' 6-1/4" and 4' 10" long, to the perimeter of the seating deck.

6. Build the planter box frame using 8d nails and construction adhesive. Cut small weep hole openings in the two 2x4s 12-3/4" long as shown in the plan. Join these to the 16-3/4" 2x4 center support.

7. Attach four corner posts, 14-1/4" long, to 2x4 runners 16-3/4" long, as shown in the plan. Check to be sure frame is square.

8. Complete planter frame assembly by nailing three 1x6s, 19-3/4" long, to the runners and center support using 6d nails.

9. Note the stagger of 21-1/4" edge members around the exterior of the planter. Start 1/4" above the bottom of the frame and attach four 2x4s using 8d nails and construction adhesive. Refer to plan.

10. Attach three more layers of 2x4 edge members around the planter frame, interlocking pieces at corner posts.

11. Join planter box and bench assemblies with their common 2x4 edge members, 4' 8-1/2" and 3' 3-1/2" long. Attach them to planter box first using 8d nails and construction adhesive. Move completed planter box into place and join edge members to 2x4 cross supports of bench.

12. Fabricate a liner for the planter box by double-bagging the two heavy-duty garbage bags. Roll down the top edges of both to form a collar of several thicknesses. From the leftover 1x6 materials, cut four tacking blocks, each about 3-1/2" long. Loosely fit the liner inside the planter, with the top collar about one inch below the rim. Nail the tacking blocks through the liner into the corner posts using 6d nails. Puncture the bottom liner in line with the spaces between the 1x6 bottom members to permit the passage of moisture.

13. Coat with water repellent sealer.

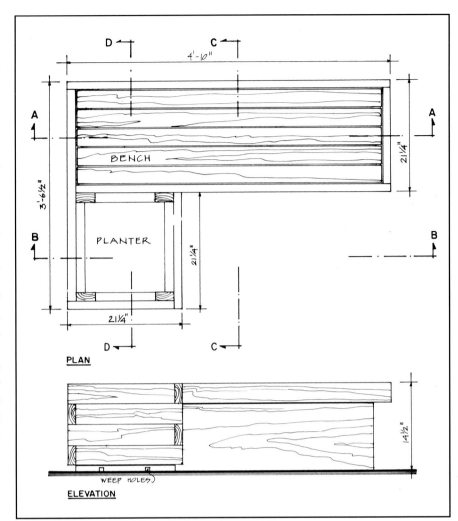

PLAN

ELEVATION

Courtesy of Southern Pine Council

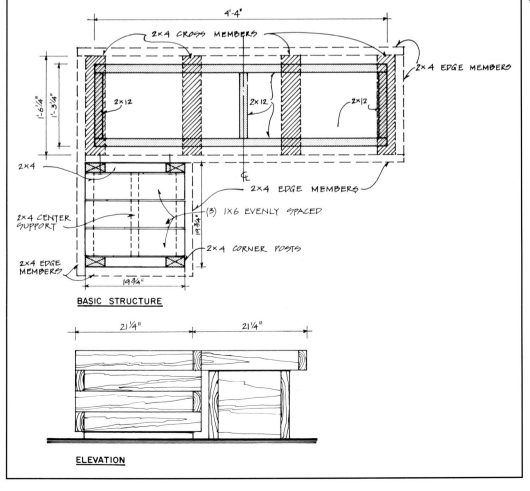

BASIC STRUCTURE

ELEVATION

49

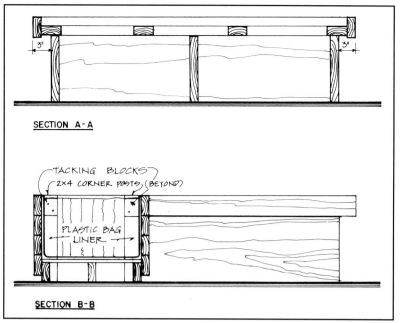

SECTION A-A

TACKING BLOCKS
2×4 CORNER POSTS (BEYOND)

PLASTIC BAG
LINER

SECTION B-B

Courtesy of Southern Pine Council

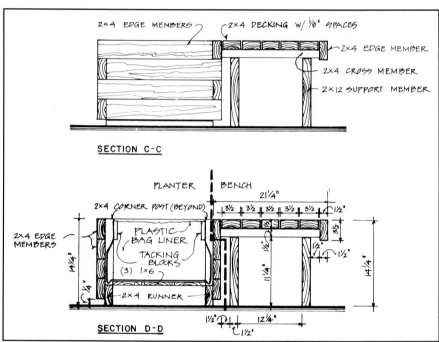

2×4 EDGE MEMBERS   2×4 DECKING W/ ⅛" SPACES

2×4 EDGE MEMBER

2×4 CROSS MEMBER

2×12 SUPPORT MEMBER

SECTION C-C

PLANTER   BENCH

21¼"
3½ 3½ 3½ 3½ 3½ 1½

2×4 CORNER POST (BEYOND)

2×4 EDGE
MEMBERS

PLASTIC
BAG LINER

TACKING
BLOCKS

(3) 1×6

14¼"

11¼"

14¼"

2×4 RUNNER

1½"   12¼"   1½"

SECTION D-D

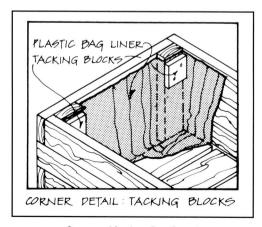

PLASTIC BAG LINER
TACKING BLOCKS

CORNER DETAIL: TACKING BLOCKS

Courtesy of Southern Pine Council

50

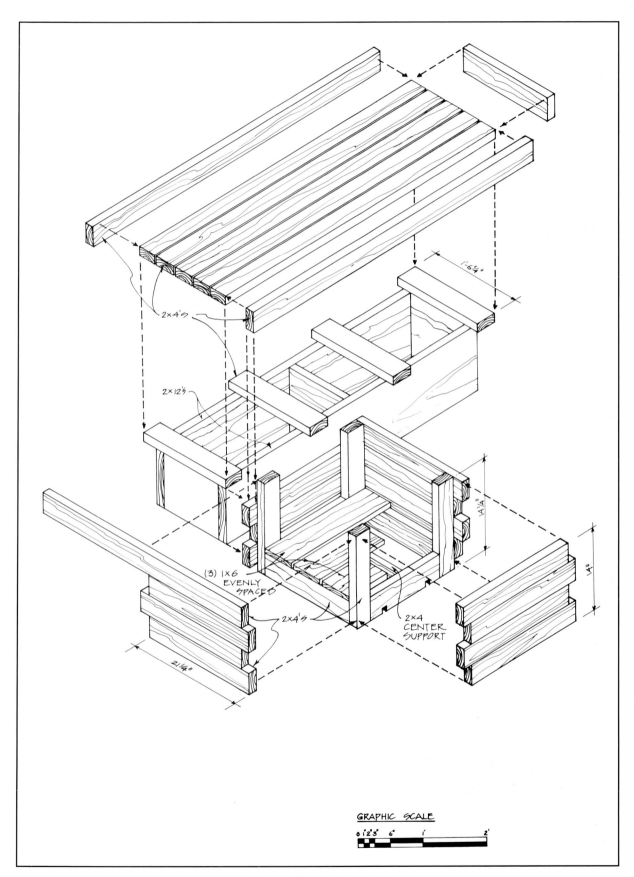

2×4's

2×12's

(3) 1×6
EVENLY
SPACED

2×4's

2×4
CENTER
SUPPORT

1'-6¼"

14¼"

14"

2¼"

GRAPHIC SCALE

0 1 2 3" 6"   1'   2'

Courtesy of Southern Pine Council

51

Mendocino Bench

Free-standing and Built-in

Courtesy of California Redwood Association

This simple yet elegant design is illustrated with options for use as free-standing or built-in-railing seating. It was designed with clean, horizontal lines and rich redwood tones to reflect the simple beauty of Northern California. Comfortable and elegant, with a gracefully curved seat and angled backrest, it offers a standing invitation to sit, relax, and enjoy.

Materials for Free-standing bench

Wood
6 2x4s at 6' for top, seat, and backrest rails
6 2x2s at 6' for seat and backrest rails
2 2x4s at 5' 9" for main braces
9 2x4s at 26" for seat and backrest supports
2 4x4s at 20-1/2" for front legs
2 4x4s at 30-1/2" for rear legs
2 4x6s at 26"

Other
1-1-1/2 pounds of 3- and 4-inch corrosion-resistant deck screws

Instructions for Free-standing Bench

1. **Armrests.** Trim the front end of each 4x6 armrest at a 45° angle, beginning 1-1/2" down from the top. Notch the inside back of each armrest where it will wrap the rear leg. Finish with a 45° bevel cut. See armrest detail.
2. **Legs.** Using 4-inch screws, attach armrests to 4x4 rear legs, 24 inches up from the bottom. Attach armrests to front legs by driving two screws through the armrest and into the top of the leg.
3. **Main braces.** Trim 2x4s for the main braces and attach to inside front and rear legs, 11 inches from bottom.
4. **Seat supports.** The curved seat supports are made up of 2x4 lumber sandwiching either the 4x4 rear legs or the single 2x4 backrest support. To shape the curve, make a template for a 36-inch radius cut. Mark the cut to start 3 inches in from the front. Use a bandsaw to cut the radius to a depth of no more than 1-1/4". Finish the seat supports with a 45° bevel cut to match the armrests.

   Note that the end and center seat supports differ slightly in length and attachments.
5. **End seat supports.** Trim four 2x4s to 25-1/2". Attach the inside seat supports to the rear and front legs so they rest on the top edge of the 2x4 main braces. Attach the outside seat supports level with the inside ones.
6. **Center seat supports.** Trim the two center seat supports to 22 inches. Using a scrap piece of 2x4 as a temporary spacer for the backrest, attach these seat supports across the main braces flush with the back edge of the rear brace. Use two 3-inch screws for each joint, angled from below and inside. Remove the spacer.
7. **Backrest supports.** Trim the 2x4 backrest supports to a 10° angle at the top edge. The two end backrest supports start at the top of the 4x4 rear leg and trim to rest on top of the seat supports. The center backrest trims flush to the bottom edges of the two center seat supports.

   Attach the end backrest supports to the inside of the 4x4 rear leg with two screws. The bottoms should fit snugly to the top of the seat supports and can be secured with screws driven at an angle from below.

   You should install the top rail before trimming and attaching the center backrest.
8. **Top rail.** Attach the 2x4 top rail to the rear legs with three deck screws at each end. Measure and trim the center backrest. Install between the seat supports and flush to the underside of the top rail. Secure with screws.
9. **Seat and backrest rails.** Trim one 2x2 backrest rail to fit between the armrests. Trim the other 2x2 and 2x4 seat

and backrest rails to six feet.

Install the front seat rail so that it overlaps the seat support by 1/2", and attach with two deck screws at each joint. Attach the rear seat rail to each support with two deck screws. Adjust the spacing of the remaining seat rails before attaching.

Space the backrest rails equally, and attach to supports with a single screw at each 2x2 and two screws at each 2x4.

Materials for Built-in Bench

Wood
6 2x4s at 4' for top, seat, and backrest rails
6 2x2s at 4' for seat and backrest rails
4 2x4s at 2' for backrest supports
2 4x4s at 26" for seat supports
4 4x4s at 11" for front and rear legs
2 4x4s at 39-1/4" for posts

Other
1 to 1-1/2 pounds of 3- and 4-inch corrosion-resistant deck screws
4 sets of machine bolts, washers, and nuts, 1/2 x 6 inches

Instructions for Built-in Bench

1. **Posts and legs.** Install the 4x4 posts with machine bolts. Each post extends from the deck framing and is attached to either the rim joist or the deck joist with two 1/2" by 6" machine bolts. See section detail.

2. **Seat supports.** Follow the instructions for the free-standing bench seat supports to measure and cut the curved seat radius. Trim all the 4x4 seat supports to 22 inches. Attach them to the front and rear legs using three 4" screws driven from the top.

3. **Backrest supports.** Trim both ends of each 2x4 double backrest support to 10°; attach flush to the top of each 4x4 post and to the 4x4 seat supports.

4. **Top rail.** Trim the 2x4 top rail to length and attach to posts with screws. Use bevel cuts at any butt joints to minimize gapping.

5. **Seat and backrest rails.** Trim 2x2 and 2x4 seat and backrest rails to length and attach as described in the freestanding bench.

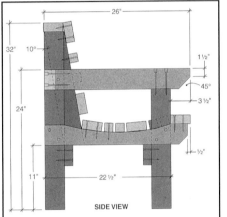

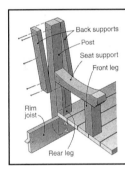

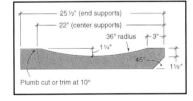

Courtesy of California Redwood Association

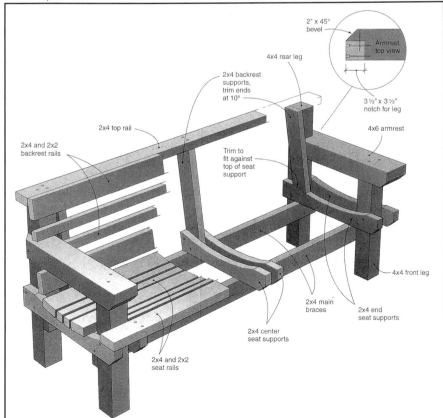

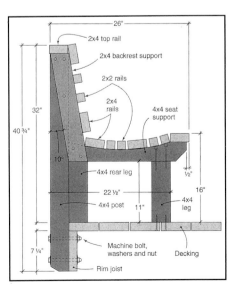

53

Butcher-block Bench

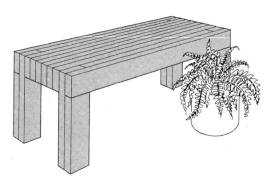

Courtesy of California Redwood Association

Courtesy of California Redwood Association

This bench is durable, stable, and practical. For the beginner craftsman, it is easy to saw and nail. For the homeowner, it makes for easy planning, with plans for different-lengths varying from four to twelve feet. Its beauty as lawn, patio, or deck ornament is born of simplicity.

To keep the seats even and level, build benches on their edge or upside down on a flat surface.

Materials

Bench length	2x4 lumber
4 feet	2 pieces at 6'
	5 pieces at 8'
6 feet	12 pieces at 6'
8 feet	10 pieces at 8'
	2 pieces at 6'
10 feet	10 pieces at 10'
	two pieces at 6'
12 feet	10 pieces at 12'
	2 pieces at 6'

8-penny and 10-penny nails

Instructions

Legs are built up with two 2x4s, one long piece and one short. Trim four long pieces so that they are 18 inches long. Trim four short pieces

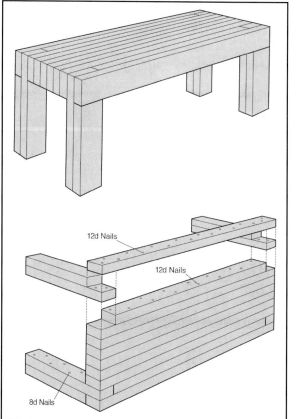

12d Nails

12d Nails

8d Nails

to 14-1/2" inches. To make legs, assemble short and long pieces in pairs with six 8-penny nails.

Seat boards are made by nail-laminating ten 2x4s together, creating the butcher-block appearance. The length of the 2x4s used for the seat will vary according to the length of the bench. (See materials lists) Trim two short pieces to accommodate the legs. Make sure the 2x4s are level and even on the top seating area. Use 12-penny nails and nail every six inches in a zigzag pattern. The seat may be planed after construction to even the seating surface.

Courtesy of California Redwood Association

Sonoma Picnic Table

Materials

For table:
5 2x6s at 60" for top slats
2 2x4s at 27" for cleats
4 2x4s at 40" for legs
2 2x4s at 30" for braces
6 sets of machine bolts, washers and nuts, 3-1/2" x 1/4"
1 pound 4-inch deck screws

For benches:
4 2x6s at 60" for top slats
4 2x4s at 11-1/2" for cleats
8 2x4s at 22" for legs
4 2x4s at 15" for braces
12 sets of machine bolts, washers and nuts, 3-1/2" x 1/4"
1 pound 4-inch deck screws

Instructions

1. **Table top.** Measure and cut the 2x6 slats. Lay the slats on a clean and stable work surface with their most attractive sides down. Separate the slats with 1/4-inch spacers and square. Clamp the slats together with a bar clamp.

2. **Cleats.** Cut the 2x4 cleats to 27 inches and trim the ends at 45° angles starting 2 inches down from each end of the table top. Allow a 3/4-inch margin from the table's edges. With the combination countersink bit, drill two screw holes into the cleat above each slat, deep enough to set the screw heads below the surface. Fasten to slats with 4-inch screws.

3. **Legs.** Cut the legs to 39 inches with 38° parallel angles top and bottom. Loosely clamp legs together at their centers with C clamps. Adjust the tension in the clamp until you can open the legs to make a cross with a 28-1/2-inch span at each side, with tops and bottoms aligned. Mark along the sides of each leg where they cross. Remove the clamp and cut the half laps from each 2x4 leg. Re-clamp the legs in position.

   Attach leg assemblies to table top cleat with two 3-1/2-inch x 1/4-inch machine bolts at each connection.

4. **Braces.** Mark and cut table braces to fit between the table leg assembly and the table top with 45° angles at both ends. Attach braces to table top with 4-inch screws from below. Drill bolt holes through the "X" of the legs and completely through the angled ends of each 2x4 brace. Countersink the bolt holes to accommodate washers and nuts. Install the bolts and remove the clamps.

5. **Bench construction.** Follow the same basic construction methods described for the table, using the dimensions given in the illustration below. Notable differences from the table design include the lengths of the legs, cleats, and braces and the angles of the crossed legs.

Courtesy of California Redwood Association

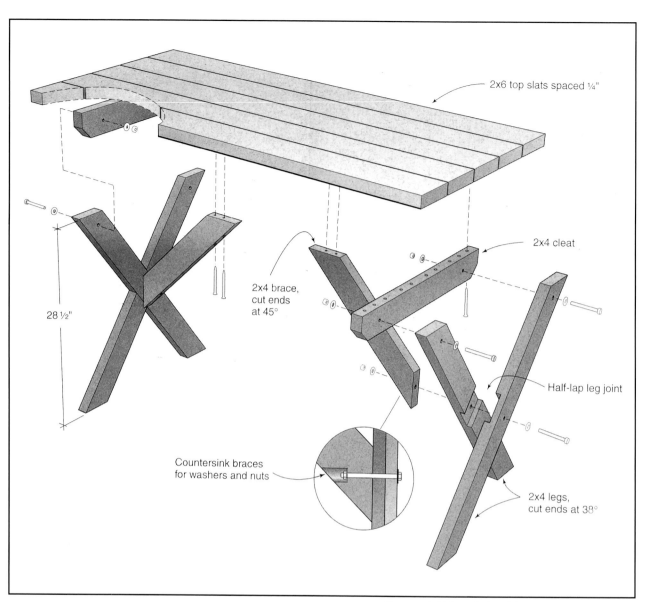

2x6 top slats spaced ¼"

2x4 cleat

2x4 brace,
cut ends
at 45°

28½"

Half-lap leg joint

Countersink braces
for washers and nuts

2x4 legs,
cut ends at 38°

Courtesy of California Redwood Association

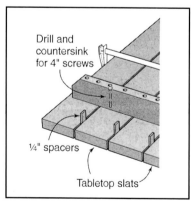

Drill and
countersink
for 4" screws

¼" spacers

Tabletop slats

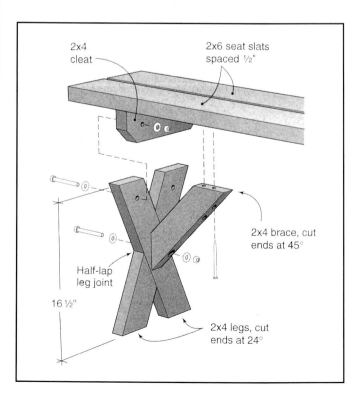

2x4
cleat

2x6 seat slats
spaced ½"

2x4 brace, cut
ends at 45°

Half-lap
leg joint

16½"

2x4 legs, cut
ends at 24°

Garden Bench

Courtesy of Georgia-Pacific

Here's a picture perfect bench designed by Georgia-Pacific, with lots of scallop work to create a charming country effect. You'll have to spend a lot of time and care, but the compliments will make it well worthwhile.

Materials

2 2x6s at 8' cut to:
    2 at 17" for side aprons, shape tops and scallop bottom edge
    2 at 6" for armrest support brackets, shape outside curves as shown
    1 at 49" for backrest, shape top as shown
    1 at 40-1/2" for front apron, scallop bottom
    1 at 40-1/2" for back apron, scallop bottom

2 2x8s at 6', cut to:
    2 at 26" armrests, shape outside edges as shown
    2 at 36" back legs, cut to 3" wide angling the top part as shown at +/- 19° angle from the vertical

5 2x4s at 8' cut to:
    1 at 40-1/2" back rail, plane to 1-1/2" x 3"
    2 at 23-1/4" for front legs, plane to 1-1/2" x 3"
    2 at 20" for side seat supports, shape tops to form a seat curve as shown
    2 at 40-1/2" for front and back seat slats
    4 at 43-1/2" for seat slats

1 1x4 at 8' cut to:
    8 12" back slats

Other

4 at 1/4" x 3-1/2" galvanized lag screws
8 at 3/8" x 3-1/2" galvanized carriage bolts with washers and nuts
60 +/- 4d 2-1/2" decking screws
1 tube waterproof construction adhesive

Instructions

1. Cut all pieces to final size, sculpt curves as necessary and sand edges smooth.
2. Attach side seat supports to front and back legs using carriage bolts.
3. Screw aprons to front, back, and sides.
4. Screw seat slats to side seat supports.
5. Rabbet backrest bottom edge and backrail top edge to admit backslats, glue in place.
6. Notch backrest and glue to rear legs; screw backrest and backrail to rear legs.
7. Notch under armrests; glue and insert front legs (screws optional).
8. Lag armrests to rear legs.
9. Screw armrest support brackets in place.
10. Paint.

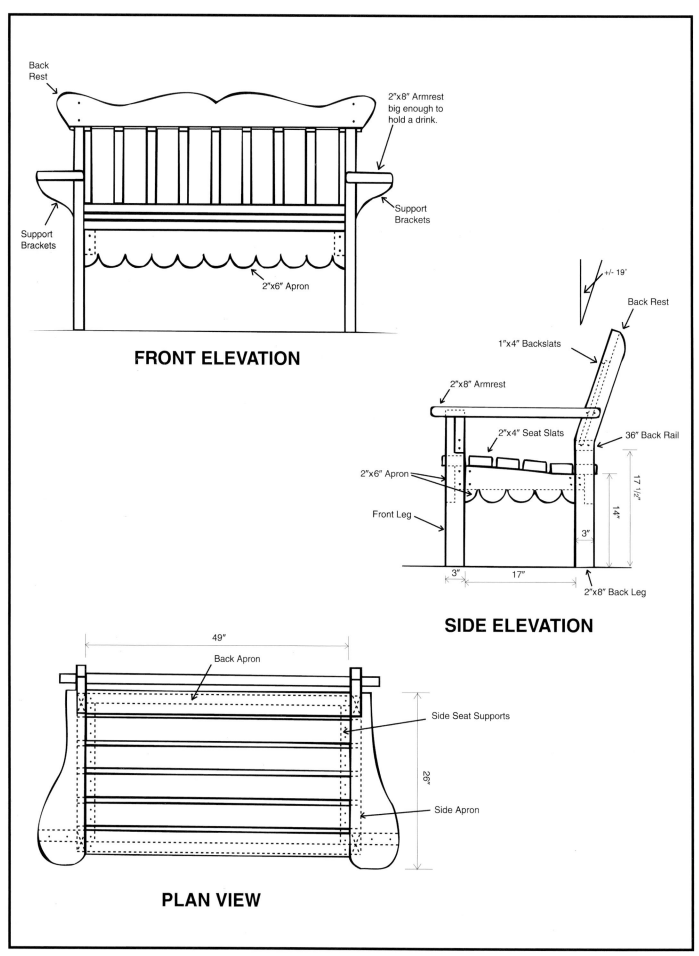

FRONT ELEVATION

Back Rest

2"x8" Armrest big enough to hold a drink.

Support Brackets

Support Brackets

2"x6" Apron

+/- 19°

Back Rest

1"x4" Backslats

2"x8" Armrest

2"x4" Seat Slats

36" Back Rail

2"x6" Apron

17 1/2"

14"

Front Leg

3"

3"

17"

2"x8" Back Leg

SIDE ELEVATION

49"

Back Apron

Side Seat Supports

26"

Side Apron

PLAN VIEW

Swing

Courtesy of Georgia-Pacific

When there's no summer breeze, you can make one for yourself with this swing. A traditional favorite for lovers and children, this double-seater promises to become a focal point for those in need of fifteen minutes solace.

Designed in the Adirondack style by Georgia-Pacific, you might want to consider a traditional approach by painting it in a bold, solid color.

A word of caution: make sure that whatever the swing is secured to can support the weight of the swing and its occupants.

Materials and Instructions

Wood

1 2x8 at 8' cut to:

> 2 26" armrests (horizontal), notch 1/2" to hold front and side arm supports. Cut a hole or shallow depression to fit your favorite cup. Curve edges.

3 2x4s at 8' cut to:

> 2 17-1/2" side seat supports. Cut tops to conform to a comfortable seat curve as shown. Cut backs at 9-1/2° angle.
> 1 52" bottom back support (horizontal). Lag bolt to side seat supports.
> 1 52" center back support (horizontal). Sand or sawcut ends to fit against armrests and screw tight to arm rests and back arm supports.
> 1 52" front seat skirt (horizontal). Cut decorative curve. Lag bolt side seat supports 2 inches from ends.
> 2 13" front arm supports (vertical). Cut decorative curve. Attach to front seat skirts with carriage bolts and nuts. Glue top edges and fit into armrest notches. Screw eyebolts for chain through armrests into arm supports.
> 2 14" back arm supports (vertical). Cut tops at 9-1/2° angle, then glue and fit into armrest notches. Screw eye bolts through armrests into arm supports as above. Trim bottom edges and lag bolt bottoms to side seat supports.

6 1x4s at 8' cut to:

> 1 48" top back support (horizontal)
> 4 48" seat slats (horizontal). Screw to side seat supports.
> Back slats: 4 30" back slats (vertical); 4 34" back slats (vertical); 2 35" back slats (vertical). Cut tops of back slats as shown and screw to all horizontal back supports.

Other

2 10' lengths of galvanized steel chain or longer to fit your porch ceiling so seat is 16" from floor.
6-3/8" x 4" eye bolts.
2-5/16" "S" hooks or clips to hold chain.
6-5/16" x 4" lag bolts with washers.
2-3/8" x 3-1/2" carriage bolts with nuts and washers.
1 box of deck screws, stainless steel or galvanized. For a finished look, recess screw heads and fill with wood plugs or putty. Water-repellent wood glue.

Finish with water repellent or semi-transparent stain or three coats of exterior paint after wood is thoroughly dry (may take several months of exposure for pressure-treated wood to dry).

For heavy use, eyebolts need glue, and add a nut by drilling to the bolt end from the side.

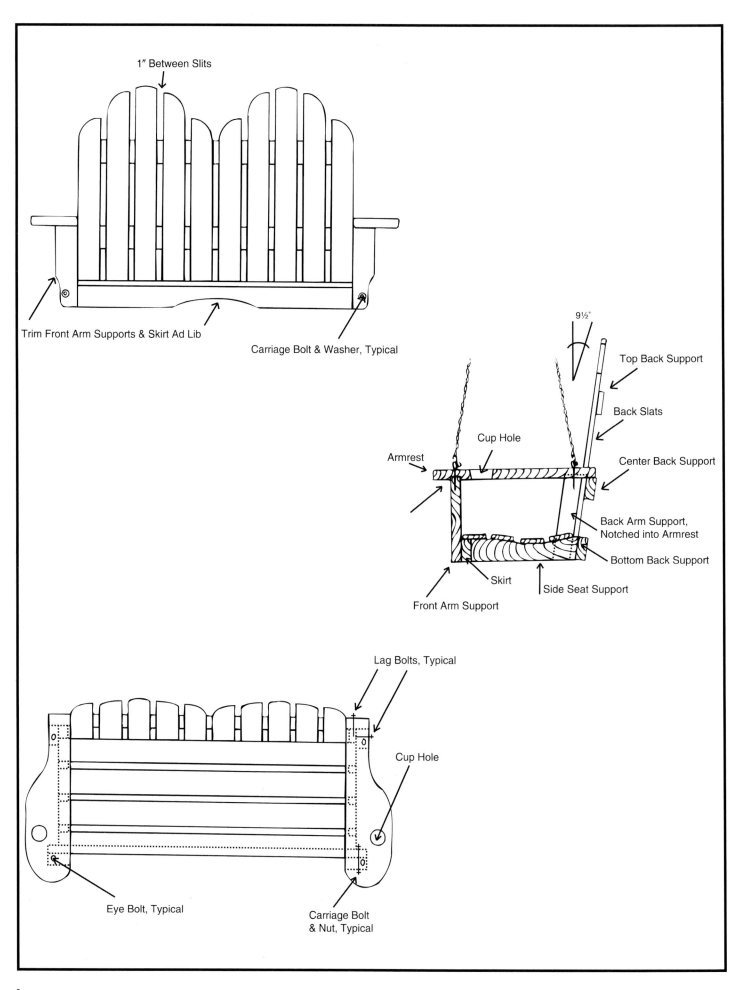

1″ Between Slits

Trim Front Arm Supports & Skirt Ad Lib

Carriage Bolt & Washer, Typical

9½°

Top Back Support

Back Slats

Center Back Support

Cup Hole

Armrest

Back Arm Support,
Notched into Armrest

Bottom Back Support

Side Seat Support

Skirt

Front Arm Support

Lag Bolts, Typical

Cup Hole

Eye Bolt, Typical

Carriage Bolt
& Nut, Typical

SHADE AND SHELTER

Arbor

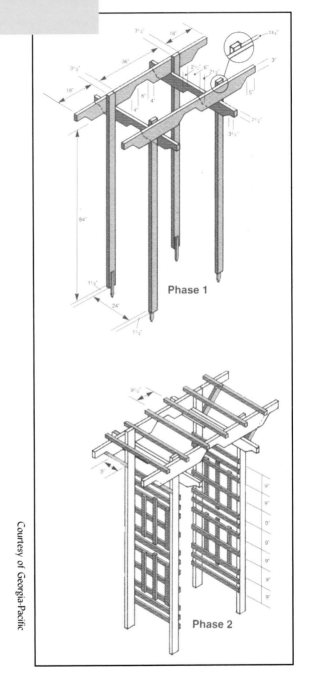

Phase 1

Phase 2

Courtesy of Georgia-Pacific

Here's a wonderful way to beautify your garden. An arbor from Georgia-Pacific creates a focal point in the yard, a small shady destination, and a place to plant ornamental, climbing plants. It can also be ornamented with hanging baskets.

Be careful, however, that no one climbs the arbor. It is not intended to support the weight of a person or any objects other than plants.

Materials

Wood

2 2x8s at 7' cut to 79" for top beams
2 2x6s at 5' cut to 51" for side beams
4 2x4s at 8' cut to 93" minimum for posts
3 2x2s at 6' cut to six 36" lengths for top plant supports
1 2x2 at 8' cut to four 19" lengths for brackets
11 1x2s at 8' cut to:
        22 27" horizontal laths
        8 19-3/4" vertical laths
        4 23" vertical laths

Other

4 stout screw eyes to hold hanging potted plants from top beam ends.

Hot-dipped galvanized or stainless-steel nails as required. Note: For better hold-down power, use galvanized screws and water-proof glue. For a finished look, recess screw heads and fill with wood plugs or putty.

Water repellent or stain with water repellent or three coats of exterior paint after wood is thoroughly dry (several months exposed to weather) will help protect your pressure-treated wood from splitting, checking, warping, and splintering.

Optional: Instead of sinking posts in ground, bolt to stakes or steel bars which are sunk firmly. If the stakes or bars disintegrate years later, they can be replaced without disturbing the plantings.

Trellis

Courtesy of Southern Pine Council

A trellis can function as a unique sunscreen. It can also be the framework for an outdoor hanging garden.

This plan, designed by Lyn Rosenberg for the Southern Pine Council, will show you how to build a 14x16 foot trellis for your garden, deck, or patio. The columns can easily be incorporated into a deck design. You can expand or reduce the modular dimensions of this trellis plan to suit your specific requirements.

When it's finished, you can plant clinging ivy or vines, add hanging baskets of flowers, and extend your garden to an overhead display of color and fragrance.

For structural stability, use one of the following options:

1) Sink columns 3 feet into the ground using concrete, gravel, or compacted soil for a free-standing trellis.

2) Incorporate the trellis with a deck, connecting columns with deck beams and/or joists.

3) Attach beams and purlins on at least two sides of the trellis, to your house or other permanent structure, using hot-dipped galvanized or stainless steel nails and/or hardware.

Materials

Wood
8 4x6s at 12' (10' if columns will not be sunk into the ground)
16 2x4s at 12' (10' if columns will not be sunk into the ground)
4 2x6s at 16'
4 2x4s at 16'
4 2x6s at 14'
19 1x4s at 6'
4 2x2s at 10'
22 2x2s at 4'

Other
6d, 8d, and 16d hot-dipped galvanized nails
Construction adhesive for pressure treated lumber
Water repellent sealer

Instructions

1. This trellis plan uses full lengths of most materials, however you will need to cut some wood as follows:
   From three 1x4s cut eight pieces 1' 8" long
   From ten 4-foot 2x2s cut 46 pieces 9" long
   Cut other 2x2 trim material after columns, beams, and purlins are erected to determine exact lengths required.
   If the columns will not be sunk 3 feet into the ground, cut the eight 4x6 timbers and the 16 2x4s to 9 feet in length.
2. Fabricate columns by centering a 12-foot 2x4 on the wide dimension of each 4x6 timber. Nail into place using 12d nails.
3. Fabricate purlins by centering 1x4 pieces along the four 14-foot 2x6s. Use two 6-foot 1x4s and one 1' 8" length on each side of a 2x6. Attach 1x4s using 6d nails and construction adhesive.
4. Locate and mark column location on 16-foot 2x6 beam members, 4-feet on center. Attach beams to both sides of columns using 12d nails and construction adhesive. Refer to plan.
5. Center 16-foot 2x4s on beams. Attach using 8d nails and construction adhesive.
6. Erect column/beam assemblies, 10-foot on center.
7. Attach purlins to center of columns, toe-nailing into columns using 16d nails. Use construction adhesive at this joint, also. Like the beam ends, ends of the purlins should extend beyond the column centerline by two feet. Refer to plan.
8. Complete trim assemblies between columns with 2x2 material. Make exact measurements between beams. Evenly space 11 2x2s across the two 10-foot spans, space 4 2x2s across the shorter spans of approximately 3' 6". Use 8d nails and construction adhesive to fabricate trim assemblies.
9. Attach trim assemblies between beams using 8d nails and construction adhesive. Align the top edge of the assembly with the bottom edge of the beams.
10. Finish with water-repellent sealer.

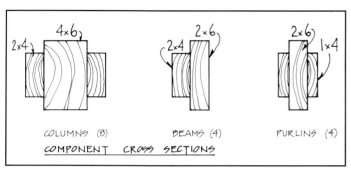

COLUMNS (8)   BEAMS (4)   PURLINS (4)

COMPONENT CROSS SECTIONS

Courtesy of Southern Pine Council

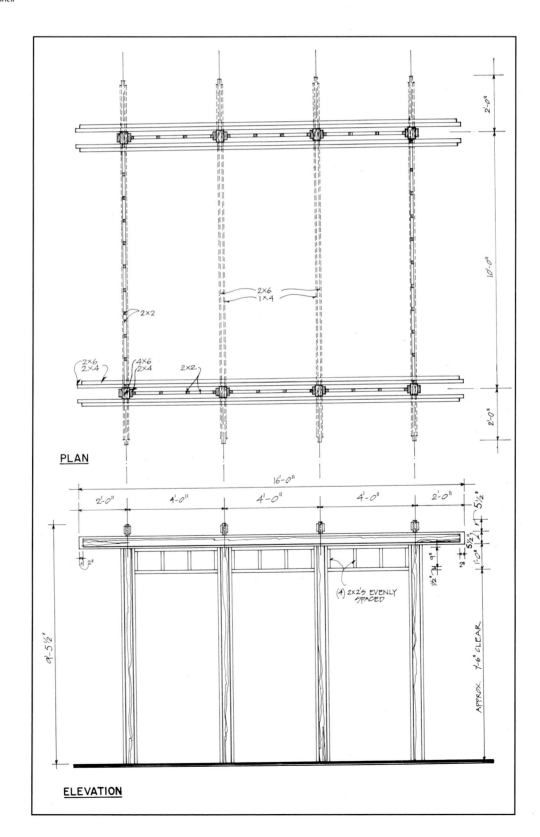

PLAN

ELEVATION

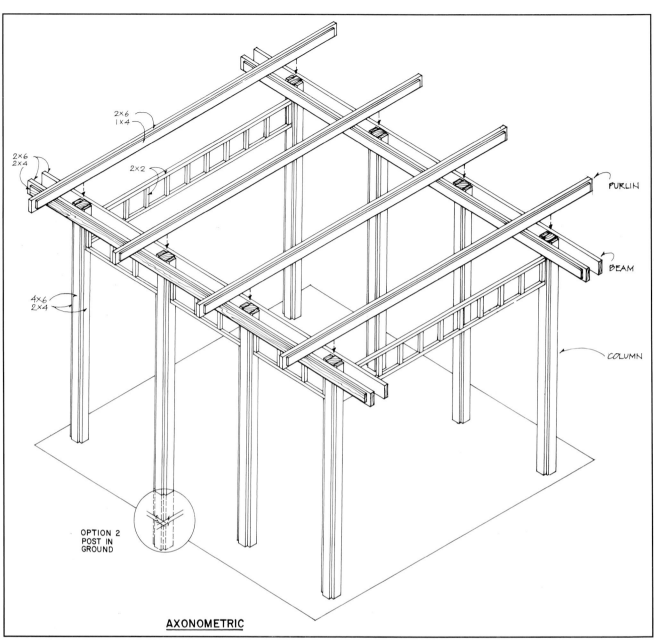

2×6
1×4

2×6
2×4

2×2

4×6
2×4

PURLIN

BEAM

COLUMN

OPTION 2
POST IN
GROUND

AXONOMETRIC

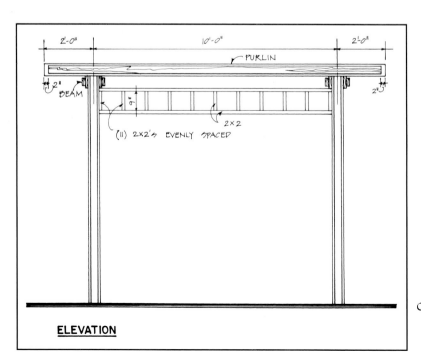

2'-0"   10'-0"   2'-0"

PURLIN

2"

BEAM

2"

9"

2×2

(11) 2×2's EVENLY SPACED

ELEVATION

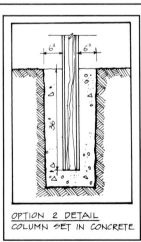

6"   6"

36"

OPTION 2 DETAIL
COLUMN SET IN CONCRETE

Courtesy of Southern Pine Council

Garden Arbor

Picture perfect, this ornamental arbor from the Southern Pine Council will draw lots of compliments. The trellis can be freestanding, on a level site, or the 2x4 posts can be set in concrete. Though you can adjust the overall height and width, if needed, the width should not exceed 4 feet.

Courtesy of Southern Pine Council

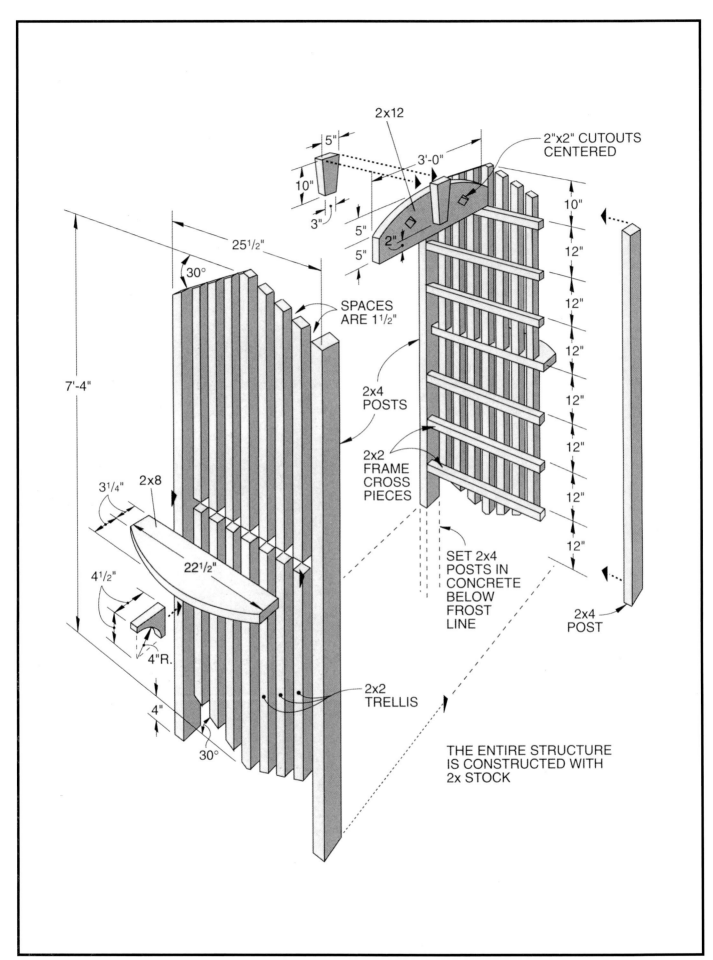

2x12

5"

10"

3"

2"x2" CUTOUTS CENTERED

3'-0"

5"

5"

2"

10"

12"

12"

12"

12"

12"

12"

12"

25½"

30°

7'-4"

SPACES ARE 1½"

2x4 POSTS

2x2 FRAME CROSS PIECES

3¼"

2x8

22½"

4½"

4"R.

4"

30°

2x2 TRELLIS

SET 2x4 POSTS IN CONCRETE BELOW FROST LINE

2x4 POST

THE ENTIRE STRUCTURE IS CONSTRUCTED WITH 2x STOCK

Courtesy of Southern Pine Council

66

Windsor Shade Shelter

This handsome shade shelter from the California Redwood Association will provide a cool place to relax in the garden or yard. The shelter can be built as a free standing unit, or attached to your home where it will keep the whole house cooler by shielding windows, walls, and sliding glass doors from the sun.

A simple weekend project, this shelter will shade an area of approximately 8 x 12 feet or 96 square feet. The basic plan can be modified by adding more posts, longer beams, and additional louvers. If you decide to enlarge this project, keep in mind that the rafters should span no more than 6 feet.

Materials

For freestanding shelter:
4   4x4s at 10-12' for posts
4   2x6s at 12' for beams
4   2x6s at 8' for rafters
23   2x2s at 12' for louvers
4   4x4s at 3' for braces
12 sets of 1/2 x 7-inch or 4-12 sets of 1/2 x 6-inch machine bolts, washers, and nuts
2 pounds of 2-1/2" deck screws
2 pounds 8d nails
Concrete and gravel as needed

For attached shade shelter
2   4x4s at 10-12' for posts
2   2x6s at 12' for beams
2   4x4s at 3' for braces
6 sets of 1/2 x 7-inch or 2-6 sets of 1/2 x 6-inch machine bolts, washers, and nuts
6-9 3/8 x 4-inch ledger lag bolts
1 tube acrylic latex or polyurethane caulking

Instructions for Freestanding Shelter

1. **Footings.** Prepare footings for the 4x4 posts which are spaced 6 feet on center and 9 feet on center. The type of footing will vary depending on the deck, patio, or type of bare ground the shelter covers. Check local building codes for footing requirements in your area. Use quick-setting concrete which hardens in about an hour.
2. **Posts.** Install or attach a 10- to 12-foot-long 4x4 post in each footing. Use a carpenter's level and temporary cross bracing – from the ground to the post – to keep the post plumb. Trim posts to final height if necessary. Posts should measure eight feet high from the surface of the ground, patio, or deck, Remove the temporary bracing once the beams and rafters are installed.
3. **Beams.** Two 12-foot-long 2x6 beams are attached to each set of posts, one on each side and extending 18 inches outward from the center line of the posts. Nail or screw the beams to position them even with the tops of the posts. Drill two half-inch diameter holes through the double beams and posts. Secure with two 7-inch machine bolts.
4. **Braces.** Cut the remaining 4x4s into four pieces, each 30 inches

long and with a 45° angle on each end. Fasten the bottom of each brace with a 6-inch machine bolt and countersink the washer and nut. The top of the brace is sandwiched between the double beams and secured with a 7-inch machine bolt.

5. **Rafters.** The 8-foot 2x6 rafters start over the posts and are spaced 18 inches on center. Toenail each rafter with 8d nails on top of the beams extending 12 inches outward front and rear. Secure the rafters with two nails driven through each side of the rafters and into each of the double beams. Screws may also be used. In either case, pre-drill to prevent splitting. Remove post bracing.
6. **Louvers.** Attach the louvers on top of the rafters with an overhang of 18 inches. Each louver is fastened from above with 8d nails or 2-1/2" screws, through pre-drilled holes, into the rafters below. Check rafter spacing with a ruler and mark each louver for drilling on the ground before installing.

Louver spacing determines the amount of shade the shelter will provide. For moderate filtered sunlight, space louvers 4 inches on center. If more shade is desired, space louvers 3 inches on center – you will require an additional 8 louvers for this spacing.

Ready-made lattice is an alternative to louvers. Lattice will provide moderate filtered sunlight in an interesting pattern. Use 2x2 supports and blocking and attach pre-assembled 4x8 lattice panels to the 2x2s with 1-inch non-corrosive fasteners. For a more finished look, frame the lattice with 1x3 fascia.

You can also design and build your own lattice pattern to meet your shade requirements.

Instructions for Attached Shade Shelter

The basic design of the redwood shelter can be modified so that it may be attached to a home. An 8-foot 2x4 ledger replaces one set of posts and double beam to support the rafters and louvers, and blocking is added between the rafters where they meet the house wall.

1. **Ledger.** Trim posts to match the height of the ledger attachment. Anchor the ledger to the house framing using 4-inch lag bolts that will pass through the ledger and into the house studs or a window or door header to provide adequate support. When connecting to a header, space bolts no more than 24 inches on center. Studs are usually spaced 16 inches on center.

Make sure there is enough room between the ledger and the eves of the house for the 2x6 rafters and louvers or other shelter material. Use acrylic latex or polyurethane caulking to seal the top joint where the ledger meets the sidewall of the house and to seal the bolts and bolt holes.

2. **Rafters and blocking.** The rafters are positioned on top of the ledger and the beams as in the freestanding version, and are toe-nailed or screwed in place. Cut to length and nail 2x6 redwood blocking between the rafters at the sidewall of the house. Seal the top edges with caulking to prevent rainwater infiltration.

Custom end details. The ends of the double beams, rafters, and louvers can be trimmed to provide a custom look. Simple shapes, while easy to create, can add elegance to your project.

Finishing. Finish your shelter with a clear water repellent or stain to enhance the natural beauty of the wood and to extend the life of your project.

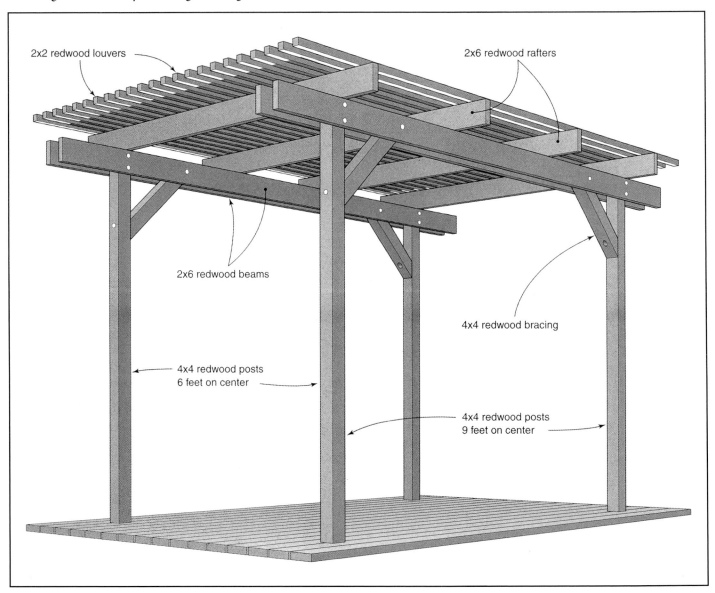

2x2 redwood louvers

2x6 redwood rafters

2x6 redwood beams

4x4 redwood bracing

4x4 redwood posts
6 feet on center

4x4 redwood posts
9 feet on center

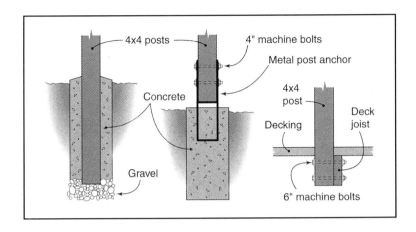

4x4 posts — 4" machine bolts — Metal post anchor

Concrete

Decking — Deck joist — 4x4 post

Gravel

6" machine bolts

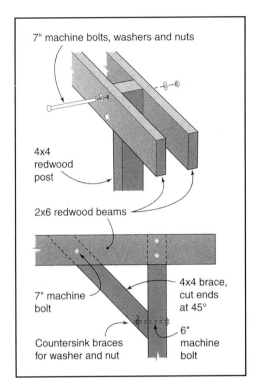

7" machine bolts, washers and nuts

4x4 redwood post

2x6 redwood beams

7" machine bolt

4x4 brace, cut ends at 45°

Countersink braces for washer and nut

6" machine bolt

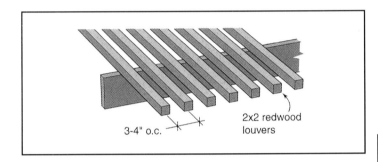

3-4" o.c.

2x2 redwood louvers

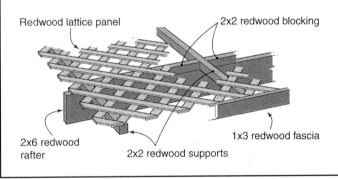

Redwood lattice panel — 2x2 redwood blocking

2x6 redwood rafter

2x2 redwood supports

1x3 redwood fascia

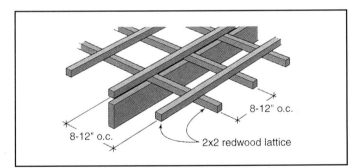

8-12" o.c.

8-12" o.c.

2x2 redwood lattice

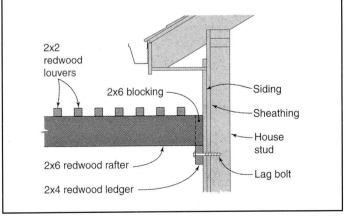

2x2 redwood louvers

2x6 blocking

Siding

Sheathing

House stud

2x6 redwood rafter

2x4 redwood ledger

Lag bolt

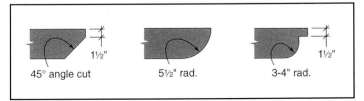

1½"

45° angle cut

5½" rad.

3-4" rad.

1½"

Courtesy of California Redwood Association

Lake Tahoe Gazebo

Courtesy of California Redwood Association

Extend your home's living space into the garden with an elegant and easy to build eight-sided redwood gazebo, a pleasant outdoor retreat for social gatherings or soothing private reflection.

This project requires careful planning and measuring during construction of each of its main components; layout, posts and footings, decking, frieze, rafters and roofing, and railings.

If you are a relative newcomer to do-it-yourself projects, follow the construction steps presented here by the California Redwood Association and seek help whenever you are unsure of the details. More experienced do-it-yourselfers will feel comfortable with this basic design and will find several areas to add personal touches. A few ideas for frieze, railing, and roofing options are offered later.

Materials

8   1x2s at 3' for batter boards
28 1x2s at 2' for wooden stakes
8   2x4s at 28 lineal feet for footing frames
8   4x4s at 10' for posts
16 1x3s at 4' for wooden braces
1   2x6 at 12'; 6 2x6s at 6'; 8 2x6s at 4'
for decking
8   2x6s at 3' for deck joist headers

184 lineal feet of 2x6s for deck boards
8   2x6s at 6' for rim joists
2   4 2x4s at 6' for lattice rails
2   3/8x4x8 panels for lattice
32 1x3s at 10-1/2" for lattice trim
1   6x6 at 7" for kingpost
16 2x6s at 9' for rafters
8   1/2" or 3/4" 4x8 panels of exterior plywood
1 roll 36" x 144' roofing felt or paper
Wood shingles as needed
16 2x4s at 6' for top/bottom rails
64 1x8s at 32-36" for slats
1 pound each of 2-1/2-, 3-, and 4-inch deck screws
2 pounds each of 16d and 10d common and 8d box or common nails
1 pound roofing nails
2 pounds roofing staples
24 2x6 joist hangers
8   4x4 post anchors
Pre-mixed concrete as needed
Gravel as needed

Roofing materials: The following measurements and quantities are guidelines only. For best results, measure and cut as you build.

For 1x4 slat roof (3-1/2" spacing)

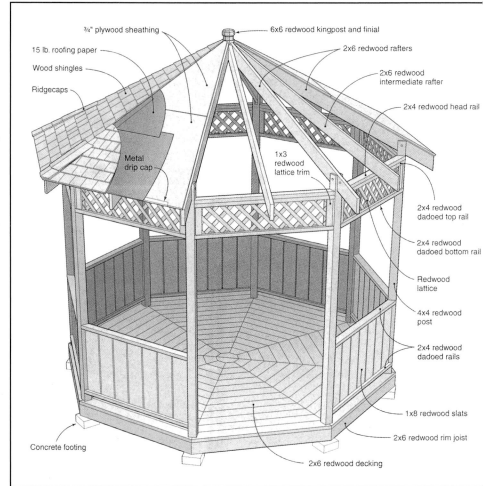

¾" plywood sheathing
15 lb. roofing paper
Wood shingles
Ridgecaps
Metal drip cap
6x6 redwood kingpost and finial
2x6 redwood rafters
2x6 redwood intermediate rafter
2x4 redwood head rail
1x3 redwood lattice trim
2x4 redwood dadoed top rail
2x4 redwood dadoed bottom rail
Redwood lattice
4x4 redwood post
2x4 redwood dadoed rails
1x8 redwood slats
2x6 redwood rim joist
2x6 redwood decking
Concrete footing

Courtesy of California Redwood Association

312 lineal feet of 1x4s for slats
12-inch square metal flashing
2 pounds 10d common nails
For 1x4 spaced sheathing (5" on center spacing)
728 lineal feet 1x4 slats
2 pounds 10d common nails
For 2x2 baluster railings
100-126 2x2s at 32" for balusters spaced 3"
32 1x1s at 5' for nailing cleats
2 pounds each, 10d common and 8d finish nails

Layout

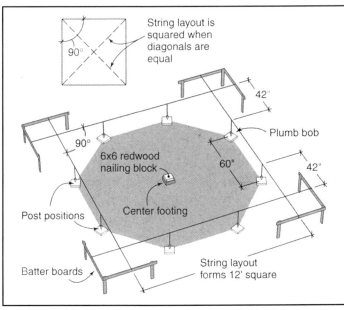

Courtesy of California Redwood Association

If you think of an octagon as a square with its corners cut off, you'll realize how simple the shape truly is. A common measurement and trim angle to remember throughout the layout and construction process is 22-1/2°. The key, as with any project, is both careful planning and precise measurement.

At a level building site, use batter boards and string to lay out a square 12 feet on each side. To check for 90° corners and to find the center of the gazebo, run strings from corner to opposite corner. The square is true and its sides are parallel when the diagonal measurements are equal.

Where the two diagonal strings cross, drive a stake into the ground to mark the position of the center footing.

Once squared, make a mark along each string 43 inches from the corner in both directions. Use a plumb bob and chalk to transfer each mark from the string to the ground, and drive a stake to mark the center of each post position. The measurement from post center to post center should be 60 inches.

Footings

Snap chalk lines from post stake to post stake to create the gazebo outline on the ground. Remove the string from one side of the layout at a time while you dig the holes for the concrete footings. Do not remove the batter boards yet, as you will need to restring the gazebo layout later to help set the post anchor bolts.

The footing holes should average 12 inches in diameter, be at least 3 feet deep and be larger at the bottom than at the opening. Fill the base of the hole with several inches of compacted gravel. In cold climates, footings should extend 6 inches below the frost line or comply with local codes.

Make 12- by 12-inch square wood frames from 2x4 lumber for each footing to contain the concrete at ground level. Restring the gazebo layout now so that the frames can be centered for positioning the anchor bolts and posts later. Level the frames to each other and use backfill or stakes to secure the frames while pouring the concrete.

Post Anchors

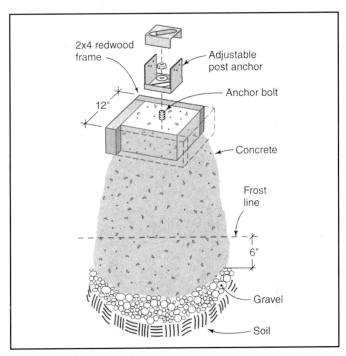

Courtesy of California Redwood Association

Use adjustable post anchors and quick-setting concrete. Pour the center footing first and set a 6-inch-long 6x6 wooden nailing block at a depth of several inches into its center so that at least four inches remain above the concrete. Trim this block to height later when framing in the deck.

Pour perimeter footings and set anchor bolts one at a time. All anchor bolts should measure six feet from the center of the gazebo and five feet from each other. Check each for plumb and level. This is important for the gazebo to properly fit together. Make any adjustments before the concrete sets completely – about half an hour.

Once the concrete is set, assemble the post anchors square to the center footing and with the required 22-1/2° angle between posts. Remove the 2x4 frames.

Posts

Cut a notch 6-3/16" deep and 1-1/2" wide in the top ends of each 4x4 post for attaching the roof rafters (see detail in rafters section). Trim the 4x4 posts to 9' 5".

Cut a double bevel of 22-1/2° beginning 5-1/2" inches from the bottom. Attach posts to footings at each metal post anchor with 10d nails. Offset the posts toward the center of the gazebo and make sure the beveled edges clear the sides of the post anchor so that the rim joists can be attached later. Plumb and brace posts.

Framing and Decking

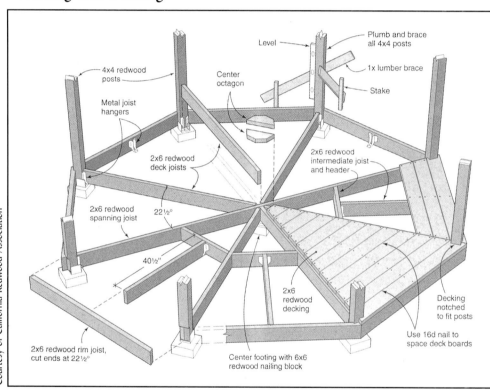

Courtesy of California Redwood Association

Deck joists. Measure and trim a single 2x6 joist to span the width of the gazebo between opposite posts. Use a string level to guide you in attaching the metal joist hangers to the posts with 10d nails. Trim the center nailing block to height so that the spanning joist will sit on it. Secure the spanning joist to the posts and toenail it to the center nailing block.

Two deck joists meet the spanning joist at 90° and are installed first, followed by four 2x6 deck joists that attach to each post. Double check these and all other joists for level.

Headers. Trim ends of 2x6 headers to opposite 22-1/2° angles. Use 16d nails to attach the headers to the deck joists where the joist span becomes greater than 24 inches and where a whole deck board will cover them.

Rim and intermediate joists. Trim 2x6 redwood rim joists with 22-1/2° opposite angles. Attach rim joists to the outside of the beveled posts with two four-inch, self-tapping deck screws per joint. Measure and trim the remaining eight intermediate joists to run from rim joists to headers. Attach with joist hangers.

Decking. Install 2x6 deck boards with two deck screws or 16d nails per bearing. If you use nails, pre-drill holes at board ends to prevent splitting.

Start the decking installation at the rim joist and notch the first row of deck boards to fit around the posts. The deck boards should trim to 22-1/2° at their ends to butt join at the centers of the deck joists.

To ensure accurate trims and spacing, lay out the first section of deck boards without trimming or nailing them. Snap chalk lines across the boards along the centers of the deck joists to mark the end cuts and nailing patterns. Use a 16d nail to space the boards. Nail heads should be flush with the board surface.

At the center of the deck, finish with a full course of deck boards and an octagon created from two halves cut from pieces of 2x6 lumber.

Frieze and Rafters

The frieze is a decorative element which can be constructed to match the railing design or a design element of the home. Since this frieze also supports some of the weight of the roof, it is constructed with a combination head and top rail.

Lattice. Ready-made 3/8" lattice panels are trimmed to 12 inches wide by the length needed – about 56 inches.

Rails. Use pre-manufactured dadoed 2x4s for the top and bottom rails. Trim all rails to length with opposite 22-1/2° angles where they attach to the 4x4 posts. Measure each post-to-post section separately, measuring from the outside edges to ensure a snug fit. Drill 3/8-inch drain holes in the bottom rails every 8 inches to prevent water damage.

Secure the head rail to the top rail with four 2-1/2" screws driven from the top rail into the head rail on both sides of the dado. Insert the lattice panel into the top and bottom rail dadoes and secure with 8d finish nails.

Assemble the frieze sections on level ground, and against a straight edge to keep them square, before toe-nailing them to the 4x4 posts. Complete the frieze with four trimmed-to-fit 1x3 boards toe-nailed to the rails with finish nails.

The sixteen 2x6 rafters join a 7-inch long octagonal 6x6 kingpost at the peak of the gazebo roof.

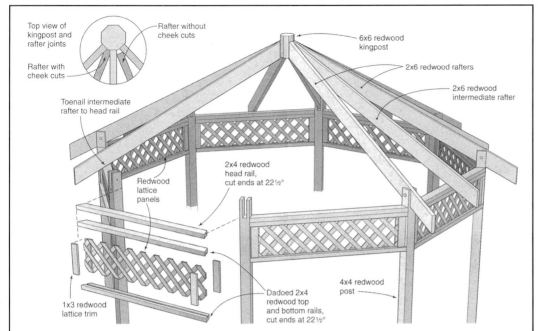

Top view of kingpost and rafter joints
Rafter without cheek cuts
Rafter with cheek cuts
Toenail intermediate rafter to head rail
Redwood lattice panels
2x4 redwood head rail, cut ends at 22½°
1x3 redwood lattice trim
Dadoed 2x4 redwood top and bottom rails, cut ends at 22½°
6x6 redwood kingpost
2x6 redwood rafters
2x6 redwood intermediate rafter
4x4 redwood post

posed design shown here, use one of the 1x4 redwood slats for 3-1/2-inch spacing. Pre-measure and carefully mark the rafters with slat positions for faster and easier installation. Snap chalk lines down the center of the rafters to guide the 22-1/2° slat-end trims. Nail the slats directly to the rafters using two 8d nails per bearing. Pre-drill holes at slat ends to prevent splitting.

Shingles over spaced sheeting. Follow the basic slat roof construction steps. Add two more slats at the roof's edge to simplify installation of the starter course. Space the rest of the slats five inches on center or to match the weather exposure. Other installation details are the same as for shingles installed over plywood sheathing.

Shingles over plywood sheathing. Each two-piece section of sheathing is cut from one 4x8 sheet of plywood. Use 8d nails to install the roof panels, allowing 1/8-inch expansion gaps at the joints. Attach metal drip caps at the eaves.

Lay and staple 36-inch wide roofing paper in layers as shown. Begin installation with the starter course made up of a double row of shingles overhanging the sheathing by 1/2 inch. Snap chalklines to ensure that additional courses are installed in straight lines. Weather exposure should be slightly less than one third the total length of the shingle. Stagger the gaps at least 1-1/2 inches above the butt line of the next course. Nails must penetrate at least 1/2 inch into the sheathing. Use longer nails on the ridge caps to penetrate the sheathing.

Ridge caps are available ready-made for easier installation or make your own. They should be trimmed to 4-5 inches wide with a 35° bevel on one edge (see detail). Install with alternate overlaps and with two nails on each side 6 to 7 inches above the butt edge. Finish at the peak with shingles trimmed to about 8 inches from the tail end.

Finial. To prevent water damage to the kingpost and rafter joint, attach metal flashing to the roof peak before toe-nailing the finial to the kingpost. Caulk the joining edges and any exposed nail heads.

Kingpost. Cut the kingpost using a table saw, or buy a readymade one. The eight main rafters trim to about 98 inches long with 26-1/2° parallel cuts.

Rafters. Attach two rafters to opposite sides of the kingpost. Center this assembly atop the gazebo with the rafters' running ends set into the post notches. Drill pilot holes through both the rafters and the posts. Secure with 4-inch bolts.

The eight intermediate rafters trim to length after installation. Cheek cut and nest them between the main rafters at the kingpost. Toenail the running ends to the head rail.

Remove bracing from the posts.

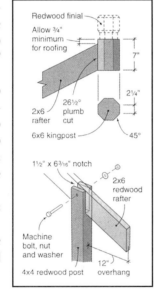

Redwood finial
Allow ¾" minimum for roofing
7"
26½° plumb cut
2x6 rafter
6x6 kingpost
2¼"
45°
1½" x 6³⁄₁₆" notch
2x6 redwood rafter
Machine bolt, nut and washer
4x4 redwood post
12" overhang

Roofing

A variety of roofing options are available and three styles are discussed here. Redwood slat roofs are economical, easy to install and offer varying degrees of protection from the sun. Wood shingles can be installed over a paper and plywood base or can be nailed directly to spaced slat sheathing which is constructed similarly to the slat roof. Shingled roofs offer full protection from the sun and rain.

Redwood slat roof. Slat size, spacing, and angle determine the amount of light and sun exposure inside the gazebo. For the fairly ex-

Railings

Custom railings and fills give a gazebo a distinct design personality because, next to the roof, they can be the most visible element. Wood railings and fills come in a few basic styles with almost limitless variation. From solid slat to cutout, from squared baluster to turned, choose a style that enhances the overall gazebo design. Follow the basic construction steps for solid slat railings or choose to use 1x1 nailing cleats as shown in the illustrations at upper right.

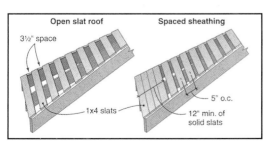

Open slat roof
3½" space
1x4 slats
Spaced sheathing
5" o.c.
12" min. of solid slats

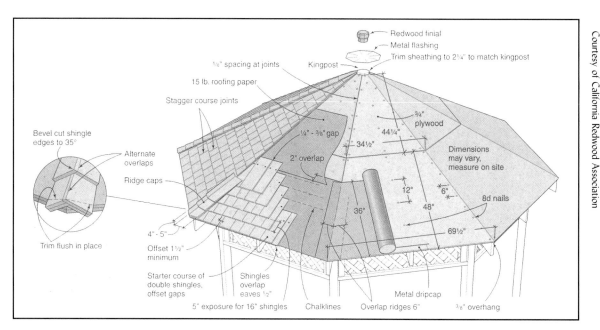

Redwood finial
Metal flashing
Trim sheathing to 2¼" to match kingpost
Kingpost
⅛" spacing at joints
15 lb. roofing paper
Stagger course joints
¾" plywood
44¼"
¼" - ⅜" gap
34½"
2" overlap
Dimensions may vary, measure on site
Bevel cut shingle edges to 35°
Alternate overlaps
Ridge caps
12"
6"
36"
48"
8d nails
69½"
Trim flush in place
4" - 5"
Offset 1½" minimum
Starter course of double shingles, offset gaps
Shingles overlap eaves ½"
Metal dripcap
5" exposure for 16" shingles
Chalklines
Overlap ridges 6"
⅜" overhang

Solid slat railings. Use ready-made dadoed redwood 2x4 rails to make railing construction easier. Nailing cleats can also be used to secure slats. Railing height from the deck surface should be 36 to 40 inches or conform to local building code.

Take the outside post-to-post measurements, and trim railing ends to 22-1/2° or to match the post angles. Drill 3/8-inch diameter drain holes every 8 inches in the bottom dadoed rails. Cut the 1x8 railing slats to at least 32 inches. Use 10d nails or 3-inch screws to attach bottom rails to the posts 4 inches above the decking. Insert the slats and cap with the 2x4 top rail secured to posts with 10d nails or 3-inch screws.

Cutout slats. This style often expands on a custom design detail from the frieze and it can be as simple as the oval pattern shown above, or as elaborate as the gingerbread designs of the Victorian era. Create a template from hardboard and transfer the pattern to the 1x8 redwood slats. Use a band or saber saw to cut the pattern from several boards at a time. Secure the redwood slats to the rails with nailing cleats.

Balusters. Squared or turned baluster railings open up a gazebo to its surroundings, while giving it both a traditional and elegant look. Ready-made, turned 2x2 balusters cost just a bit more than the squared balusters and some suppliers also offer matching posts. With the proper tools,

you can create your own custom balusters of simple or ornate design. Use dadoed rails or nailing cleats to secure the balusters, and space balusters no more than 4 inches apart for safety.

You can also assemble baluster-style railings without using nailing cleats or dadoed rails. Drive 8d nails up through the bottom 2x4 rails into the baluster bottoms, and then carefully toenail the top of the baluster to the top rail, hiding the nail heads.

Nailing options. The detail shows two options for constructing slat or baluster railings with 1x1 molding used as nailing cleats.

Sanding and finishing. Sand railings with medium grit sandpaper. Apply a water repellent finish.

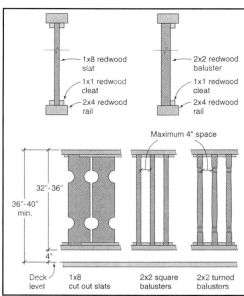

1x8 redwood slat
1x1 redwood cleat
2x4 redwood rail

2x2 redwood baluster
1x1 redwood cleat
2x4 redwood rail

Maximum 4" space

32"-36"
36"-40" min.
4"

Deck level
1x8 cut out slats
2x2 square balusters
2x2 turned balusters

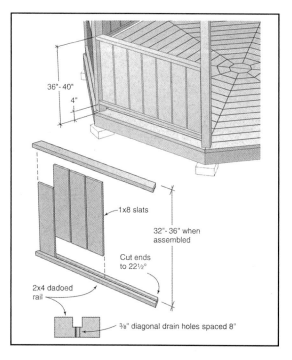

36"-40"
4"

1x8 slats
32"-36" when assembled
Cut ends to 22½°
2x4 dadoed rail
⅜" diagonal drain holes spaced 8"

Square Gazebo

A gazebo is more than just an outdoor shelter. It can function as a backyard retreat for those warm summer afternoons, a casual dining area, or as a gathering spot for friendly neighbors.

This gazebo plan by Norberto F. Nardi, AIA, for the Southern Pine Council, includes several options you may or may not want to include in your project. It's a flexible design that can be built as detailed here, or tailored to suit your home's architectural style. The individual privacy screen sections can be screened for better protection from insects.

Courtesy of Southern Pine Council

Materials

8   4x4s at 10'
1   6x6 at 2'
15   2x6s at 14'
16   2x6s at 10'
16   2x8s at 12'
2   2x8s at 14'
2   2x12s at 12'
1   2x12 at 8'
30   2x4s at 12'
26   1x6s at 12' (specify Southern Pine radius edge decking, premium, R.E.D. or R.E.D. grade.)
80   2x2s at 8'
8 sheets 4x8, 3/4"-thick pressure treated plywood for roof sheathing
8d, 10d, 12d, and 16d hot-dipped galvanized nails
Concrete for four footings, each 18" x 27" x 6".
8   4x4 post anchor bases
Water repellent sealer
Construction adhesive for pressure-treated lumber
Roofing materials to cover 160 square feet, including fiberglass or asphalt shingles, roof felt (15 pounds), and roofing nails

Instructions

1. Determine exact location of the gazebo. Use stakes, line, and level to locate positions of concrete footings. Excavate an area sufficient for 18" x 27" x 6". Pour footings and install 4x4 post anchor bases before concrete sets. Allow sufficient time for concrete to set; follow the concrete mix manufacturer's directions.

2. Position pairs of 10-foot 4x4 posts in the anchor bases at the corners. Attach bases to posts using 12d nails. To stabilize the posts, attach the front 2x6 beam (use a 14') that will support ceiling joists, so that the top edge of the beam is 5-1/2" from the top of the 4x4 post. Repeat this procedure across the rear posts. Check for level and square. Refer to plan.

3. Add the two end 2x6 ceiling joists (use 14" material to provide 3-1/2" overhang), fitting them between 4x4 posts and resting on 2x6 beams. Toe-nail to posts using 12d nails. Be sure frame remains level and square.

4. Similarly, install a 14-foot 2x8 and beam between the 4x4 corner posts on either side. Top edge of beam should be 1" below finished deck surface. Toe-nail to posts using 12d nails. Trim overhang to 3-1/2" beyond posts.

5. Build two triple 2x8 beams with 2x2 ledger to support floor deck. Use 10d nails and construction adhesive to build triple 2x8 beam, and to attach ledger to bottom inside edge. Each beam should be 11' 2" long. Install beams to inside of 4x4 posts front and rear; top edge is flush with top of 2x8 beams. Attach to end beams and posts using 12d nails and construction adhesive. Check again for level and square.

6. Complete floor framing. Install eight 2x8 floor joists 16" on center. Notch each to rest on 2x2 ledger. Toe-nail to 2x8 beams front and rear using 12d nails. Add 2x8 bridging along the centerline of floor joist span; install with 10d nails. Floor framing is complete.

7. Attach 1x6 deck boards to floor joists. Start flush with one 2x8 and beam; trim all ends flush with the opposite end beam. Remember to nail decking "bark side up" with annual rings arching upward.

8. Using 2x4 material, attach a ledger to the 2x8 floor beams on all four sides, except at door opening, using 10d nails. Position top of 2x4 ledger 1-1/2" below deck surface. This ledger will support privacy screen wall sections.

9. Install 2x4 bench support on the two sides. Attach 2x4 between 4x4 posts so that top edge is 14-1/2" above deck surface. Toe-nail to posts using 10d nails.

10. Build side wall privacy screens. Begin by building 2x4 frame to fit inside the area defined by the 4x4 corner posts, the 2x6 end ceiling joist, and the 2x4 ledger installed in Step 8.

   Equally divide the screen width into thirds and install 2x4 vertical supports at these marks. Mark 2' 6" from the top of the screen frame and attach 2x4 horizontals at this mark between the verticals, toe-nailing with 10d nails. Cut 2x2s to fit between these horizontals, equally spacing nine 2x2s, 4-1/2" on center, between the 2x4 verticals. Align with inside edge of 2x4 frame. Attach with 10d nails.

   Using the same spacing and alignment, attach 2x2s, each 1' 3" long to bottom 2x4 frame member. Lift wall section into place between 4x4 posts. Tops of 2x2s at the bottom will now be nailed to outside of 2x4 bench support. Use 10d nails. Attach 2x4 wall frame to posts and ledger with 10d nails.

11. Cut 2x12 benches to fit between 2x4 verticals of privacy screen. Use scrap 2x8 material to cut two bench braces per seat. Refer to plan for details and locations. Install bench and braces using 10d nails and construction adhesive.

12. Build the rear screen section. Construct a 2x4 frame for the opening as described in Step 10. Add 2x4 horizontals between the verticals at a level even with the benches. Equally space 2x2s within all openings, 4-1/2" on center, as shown on the plan. Nail and toe-nail into place using 10d nails. Lift wall into position between rear posts; attach 2x4 frame to posts and ledger using 10d nails.

13. Similarly, build the front wall screen, creating a 3' by 7' door opening at the center. The opening can be left square or pointed (as shown on the plan). Use 2x4 material to frame the door. Attach completed wall section to posts and ledger using 10d nails.

14. Complete roof framing. Using five 14-foot 2x6s, install ceiling joists to rest on 2x6 beams front and rear. Joists

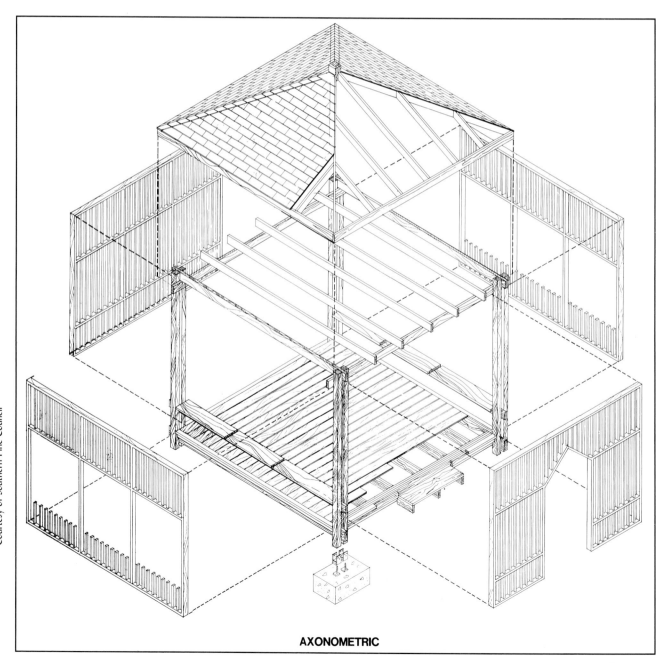

AXONOMETRIC

should be spaced equally, approximately 1' 11" on center. Taper at least 2" off the top and corners of the 6x6 piece for use as a roof peak. Use the 10-foot 2x6 material for all rafters. Cut four 2x6s to serve as ridge rafters, consider-

ing the roof slope. Refer to plan. Add center rafters square to each side of the 6x6 peak, then intermediate rafters in line with the ceiling joists. Front and rear rafters are trimmed 1-1/2" short of ceiling joist ends (which overhang 3-1/2" beyond 4x4 posts). Side rafters extend beyond 2x6 end ceiling joists and are trimmed 3-1/2" beyond the outside face of the 4x4 posts. Using 14-foot 2x6 material, attach roof fascia to all rafter ends using 10d nails. Roof framing is complete.

15. Complete roof by nailing 3/4" plywood sheathing to all rafters; use 8d nails. Add roof felt and shingles

16. If needed, build a front step using 2x12 material.

17. Construction is complete. Apply a coat of water repellent sealer to all exposed wood surfaces.

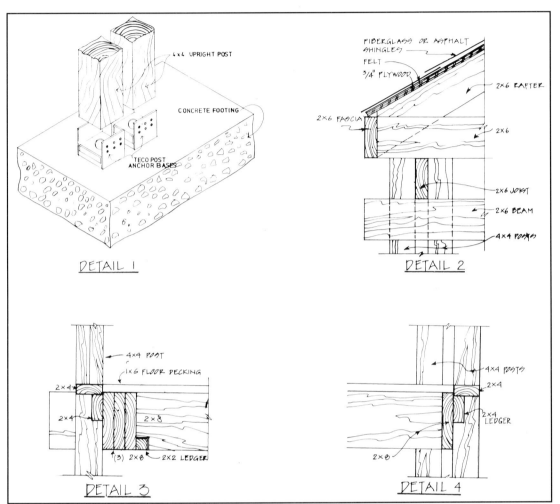

DETAIL 1

- 4 x 4 UPRIGHT POST
- CONCRETE FOOTING
- TECO POST ANCHOR BASES

DETAIL 2

- FIBERGLASS OR ASPHALT SHINGLES
- FELT
- 3/4" PLYWOOD
- 2x6 RAFTER
- 2x6 FASCIA
- 2x6
- 2x6 JOIST
- 2x6 BEAM
- 4x4 POSTS

DETAIL 3

- 4x4 POST
- 1x6 FLOOR DECKING
- 2x4
- 2x4
- 2x8
- (3) 2x8
- 2x2 LEDGER

DETAIL 4

- 4x4 POSTS
- 2x4
- 2x4 LEDGER
- 2x8

Courtesy of Southern Pine Council

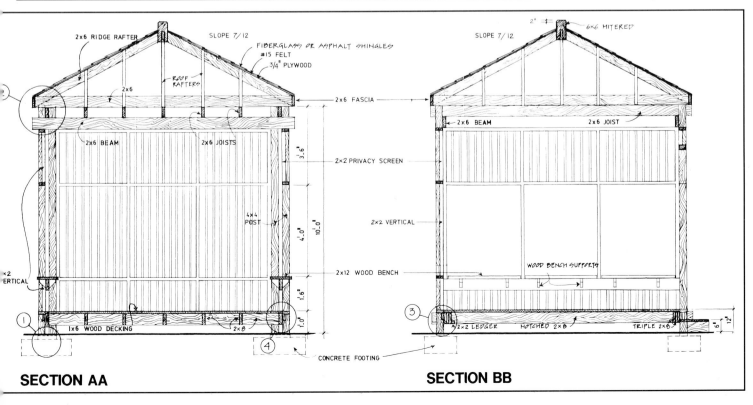

SECTION AA

- 2x6 RIDGE RAFTER
- SLOPE 7/12
- FIBERGLASS OR ASPHALT SHINGLES
- #15 FELT
- 3/4" PLYWOOD
- ROOF RAFTERS
- 2x6
- 2x6 FASCIA
- 2x6 BEAM
- 2x6 JOISTS
- 2x2 PRIVACY SCREEN
- 4x4 POST
- 2x2 VERTICAL
- 2x12 WOOD BENCH
- 1x6 WOOD DECKING
- 2x8
- CONCRETE FOOTING
- 3'-6"
- 4'-0"
- 10'-0"
- 1'-6"
- 1'-0"

SECTION BB

- SLOPE 7/12
- 2" 6x6 MITERED
- 2x6 BEAM
- 2x6 JOIST
- 2x2 PRIVACY SCREEN
- 2x2 VERTICAL
- WOOD BENCH SUPPORTS
- 2x2 LEDGER
- NOTCHED 2x8
- TRIPLE 2x8
- 6"
- 12"

SIDE ELEVATION

All overhangs 3½"
2×4 ledger under all side walls

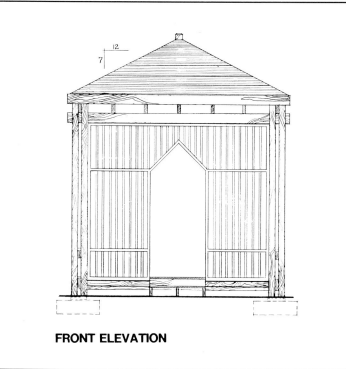

FRONT ELEVATION

12
7

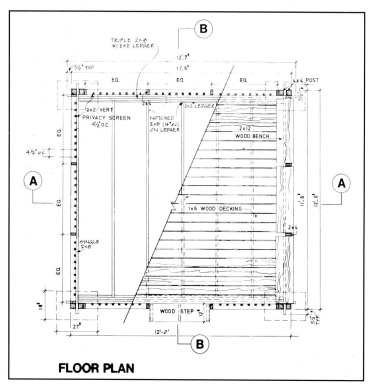

TRIPLE 2×8 W/ 2×2 LEDGER
12'-7"
11'-6"
3½" TYP
EQ. EQ. EQ.
4×4 POST
2×2 VERT. PRIVACY SCREEN 4½" O.C.
2×4
2×2 LEDGER
NOTCHED 2×8 (16" O.C.) ON LEDGER
WOOD BENCH
EQ.
4½" O.C.
2×12
1×6 WOOD DECKING
11'-6"
12'-0"
A — A
EQ.
2×4
SINGLE 2×8
EQ.
18"
WOOD STEP
12"
27"
12'-0"
5½" TYP
B

FLOOR PLAN

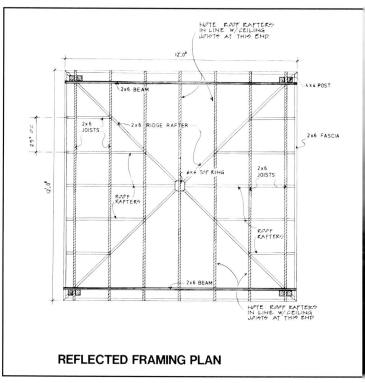

NOTE: ROOF RAFTERS IN LINE W/ CEILING JOISTS AT THIS END
12'-0"
2×6 BEAM
4×4 POST
2×6 JOISTS
2×6 RIDGE RAFTER
2×6 FASCIA
25½" O.C.
6×6 TOP RING
2×6 JOISTS
12'-0"
ROOF RAFTERS
ROOF RAFTERS
2×6 BEAM
NOTE: ROOF RAFTERS IN LINE W/ CEILING JOISTS AT THIS END

REFLECTED FRAMING PLAN

Courtesy of Southern Pine Council

Bluebird Nesting Box

The nesting box pictured here was designed specifically for bluebirds and allows for easy access for observation and cleaning. These bluebird box plans and specs were created in conjunction with the North American Bluebird Society and Georgia-Pacific.

Materials

23/32" Georgia-Pacific B-C plywood panel 24" x 24" precut
1-3/4" galvanized nails or screws, approximately 20
2 1-3/4" galvanized screws or nails for pivot point
Double-headed nail for holding door closed

Instructions

* Never put a perch on a bluebird box.
* Drain holes should be provided in the floor to allow drainage should water get in the nest.
* Small ventilation holes should be drilled in each side to provide a cross draft. Dropping the side panel down by 1/4" from the roof (see illustration) will also allow sufficient ventilation.
* Roughen up the inside front wall below the entrance hole so the young birds can "get a grip" when they try to exit the box.

Painting

The nesting box should be painted with opaque stain or primer and acrylic latex paint. Use light colors only to prevent overheating. Paint only the outside of the box. Do not use treated wood, paints that contain lead, or wood preservatives.

Location

Bluebird boxes should be placed in open areas that contain short grass with a few scattered trees and shrubs. Golf courses, cemeteries, pastures, and open meadows provide ideal habitats for bluebirds. House Sparrows can be discouraged from using a bluebird box if it is placed at least 1/2 mile from areas where sparrows congregate (urban areas and farm yards).

Courtesy of Georgia-Pacific

Monitoring Tips

* Check your bluebird houses once a week during the nesting season. After the young are 12 to 14 days old, do not open the box because they may fledge prematurely.
* Remove all House Sparrow nests.
* Become familiar with bluebird nests. They are usually constructed from grass or pine needles. The female lays 4 to 5 blue eggs and incubates them for about 14 days. The young remain in the nest for 18 to 21 days.
* Clean out the nest as soon as the young fledge.
* Keep records of the activity on your bluebird trail.
* Don't be discouraged if your boxes are not used the first year. It may take them a few seasons to find your box.
* In areas where Tree Swallows are abundant, boxes can be paired. By placing two boxes 5-25 feet apart, both species can be accommodated.

Mounting

By using the small holes shown in the top and bottom extensions of the backboard, the box may be nailed or screwed to the top or side of a wooden post, or it may be bolted or wired to the top or side of a metal post. A smooth metal post such as a galvanized pipe is preferred to a wooden post since it offers better protection against climbing predators. Boxes can be further protected by placing baffles below the box or by covering the pole with carnauba wax. Bluebird nesting boxes should be mounted at a height of from 38" to 58", higher where there is danger of vandalism. They should be set out by late winter. If possible, face away from prevailing wind and toward a single tree or shrub.

Maintenance

All boxes should be inspected, cleaned and repaired in the late fall or early winter. Bluebirds begin their nesting cycle in March.

For more information on bluebirds, to obtain The Getting Started with Bluebird fact sheet, or to set up a bluebird trail, visit the North American Bluebird Society (NABS) at www.nabluebirdsociety.org.

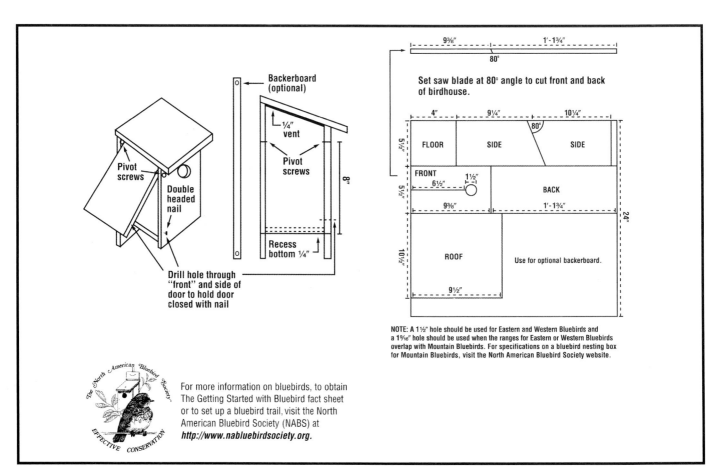

Set saw blade at 80° angle to cut front and back of birdhouse.

Recess bottom 1/4"

Drill hole through "front" and side of door to hold door closed with nail

NOTE: A 1½" hole should be used for Eastern and Western Bluebirds and a 1⁹⁄₁₆" hole should be used when the ranges for Eastern or Western Bluebirds overlap with Mountain Bluebirds. For specifications on a bluebird nesting box for Mountain Bluebirds, visit the North American Bluebird Society website.

For more information on bluebirds, to obtain The Getting Started with Bluebird fact sheet or to set up a bluebird trail, visit the North American Bluebird Society (NABS) at *http://www.nabluebirdsociety.org.*

Courtesy of Georgia-Pacific

Plywood Siding Doghouse

The Georgia-Pacific doghouse is designed to be built by the moderately experienced carpenter. The doghouse is designed to provide a sturdy shelter for a medium-sized dog. A rear vent can be added to the back side of the doghouse for additional ventilation.

Materials

Wood

From 2 2x4s at 8' cut: two front and rear bases, each 30" long; one center floor joist at 33" long; two side bases, each 33" long

From 3 2x4s at 8' cut one roof ridge brace 36" long; four corner studs at 24-1/4" tall, cut 45° miter on one end of each; four fascias at 28" long, cut 45° miter on one end of each

From 1 15/32" x 4' x 4' B-C grade plywood cut: one floor, 30" x 36"

From 2 19/32" x 4' x 8' T1-11 plywood siding with 4" on center grooves cut: two side sidings at 22-1/2" high x 36" wide; one front and rear siding at 38" high x 31-1/4" wide; one roof at 28-7/8" x 42"; one roof at 29-1/2" x 42"; one sign at 3-5/8" x 10" (cut in grooves)

From 1 1x2 at 8' cut: two doorjamb casings at 15", cut miter at 22-1/2°; two door head casings at 10", cut miters at 22-1/2° and 45°; one door sill casing at 11"; one threshold at 11"

Other

Metal flashing pre-bent at 90° angle, cut to 42" length
Galvanized finish nails
Galvanized deck screws
Wood glue
Primer, and acrylic latex paint or exterior opaque stain.

Instructions

1. Before cutting, draw layout on plywood as shown, centering front and rear siding on grooves.
2. Nail baseboards together, lapping front and rear over sides. Add a central joist at mid-span (refer to illustration).
3. Screw plywood floor on top of base.
4. Screw sides to short side of corner studs, lapping the siding 2" over the bottom of the studs. Leave 1/2" of the top of the stud exposed.
5. Screw back and front siding to corner studs, lapping front and rear over sides.
6. Add roof ridge brace by nailing through the front and back siding flush in the angle of the peak.
7. Set the assembly over the base. Screw together.
8. Nail fascia through plywood to corner studs. Screw siding to fascias from inside.
9. Screw roofs to fascias and ridge brace, lapping larger roof over smaller at ridge.
10. Nail flashing over ridge.
11. Nail casing around door as shown.
12. Nail sill flush with floor.
13. Nail threshold to cover the crack at sill and floor.
14. Paint exterior as you like.

Courtesy of Georgia-Pacific

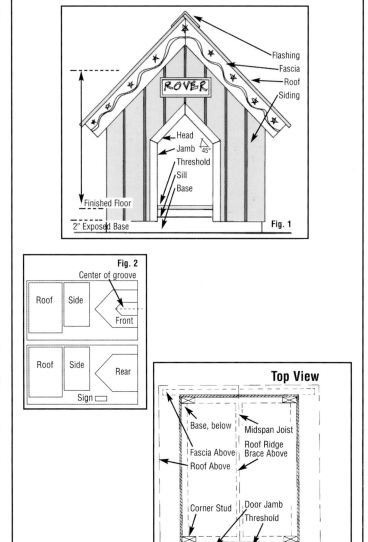

Courtesy of Georgia-Pacific

81

American Gothic Doghouse

This doghouse incorporates a little fancy carpentry work for a favorite family pet. It was designed by the Southern Pine Council to accomodate dogs up to 40 pounds, so the dimensions will have to be adjusted if your dog is larger.

When you're finished assembling the house, paint it white. Use roofing nails to attach 15-pound felt and green shingles to the roof.

Courtesy of Southern Pine Council

Courtesy of Southern Pine Council

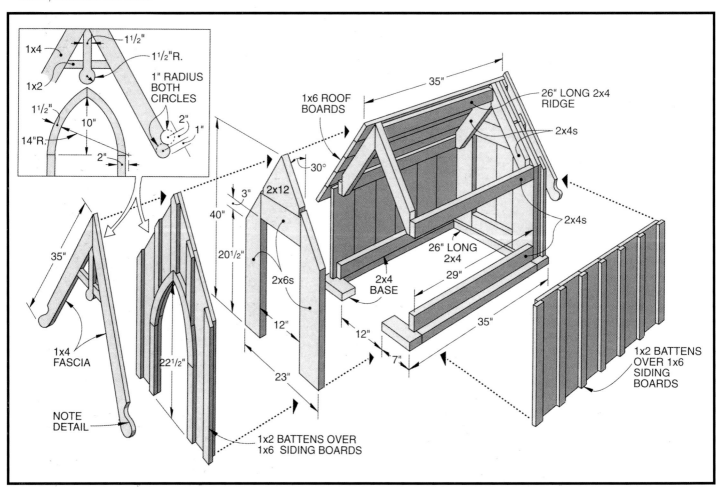

82

DECKS

Deck Around a Hot Tub

Decks turn backyards into garden retreats and the addition of hot tubs makes them even better, says the California Redwood Association. Building a deck for a tub is very much like building any other deck. The most important thing to remember is that water is *extremely* heavy and the tub will need support independent of the deck.

The major elements for this deck around a tub are:

Footings Concrete pillars or pier blocks which support the weight of the entire deck.

Posts Vertical supports for the deck attached to footings by drift pins or by toenailing. Bottoms of posts should be inches off the ground.

Stringers straddle the posts and are attached with carriage bolts or lag screws.

Joists are horizontal supports nailed to stringers 2' on center, with 16d nails which support the decking. Blocking may be nailed between joists for stabilization.

Decking is the surface of the deck. Nail with one 16d nail per joist bearing in a staggered nailing pattern. Allow 1/8" space between deckboards for drainage.

Raised seating area can also serve as storage and can conceal plumbing. The basic element is the *wall unit* which rises 24" above the deck. The decking should be 1/2" below the tub rim. Build the five wall units first and then attach the other members following standard nailing methods in this order: ledgers, joists, blocking, facing and then decking.

The access hatch consists of 2x4s or 2x6s attached to a simple box frame. The frame should measure approximately 22-1/4" x 20-3/4" so that it fits securely into the stud wall. Although the hatch can be removable, a hinge is the easiest way to attach it to the stud wall unit.

Deck Materials

Description	Quantity	Size	Length
Posts	9	4x4	height of deck
Stringers	4	2x10	16'
	2	2x10	7'
	2	2x10	2'
Joists	6	2x6	12'
	1	2x6	7'
	6	2x6	26"
Blocking	12	2x6	2'
Angle Braces	4	2x6	3'
Headers	2	2x6	8'
	2	2x6	16'
Decking		2x6	240 lin. ft.
Trim		1x2	56 lin. ft.

Raised Seating Area Materials

Description	Quantity	Size	Length
Plates	2	2x4	12'
	4	2x4	8'
Studs	21	2x4	2'
Joists	2	2x6	12'
	5	2x6	4'
	2	2x6	3'
	2	2x6	2'
Ledgers	2	2x6	6'
Facing		1x6	124 lin.ft.
Decking		2x6	124 lin.ft.

Other Materials

Nails, 5 pounds of 16d common, 12 lbs. of 16d box (all nails non-corrosive) 36 3/8"x4" lag screws and washers

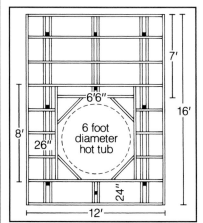

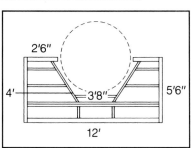

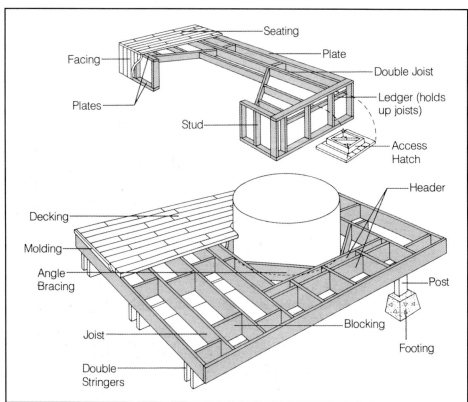

8x10 Deck

Courtesy of California Redwood Association

This small deck designed by the California Redwood Association can make a big difference at a garden doorway, next to a retaining wall or under your favorite tree. It's relatively easy to build and won't cost too much either.

1. **Placement**. First decide the placement and height of the deck. You can build a free-standing deck or one that is attached to the side of your house.

    Note: The deck described here is free-standing. To attach the deck to a house, anchor one of the skirtboards to the house framing with the simplest anchoring system permitted by local building codes.

    If the deck is adjacent to a house, it should be about one inch below the interior floor or a comfortable step down, usually about 7".

2. **Corners**. Mark the deck corners with stakes and string. Check the squareness of the projections by measuring between stakes. Then measure diagonally between the corners. If the two diagonal measurements are equal, the corners of the deck are properly marked.

3 **Posts**. Place the posts in position. If you are using a ledger on the side of the house, you will need three posts. For a free-

standing deck, you will need six. Post lengths will vary according to the contour of the ground. Establish the height at one corner and use this to measure the others. Accurate measurement and trimming of the posts can be achieved using a string level or a carpenter's level. Post tops should be 1-1/2" below the top of the skirtboards. This provides room for the deckboards. Toenail posts to the nailing blocks or pre-cast concrete footings.

4. **Skirtboards**. Attach the 2x4 ledgers to the two 8' skirtboards with 3/8" x 2-1/2" lag screws. The ledgers will support the ends of the decking. Bolt the skirtboards to the posts with 3/8" x 6" carriage bolts, washers and nuts.

5. **Joists**. Attach 2x8 joists using metal joist hangers. Leave room so that the decking will be even with the top of the skirtboards. Space the joists 24" on center, which means the center of one joist is 24" from the next.

6. **Decking**. Lay the 26 2x4 deckboards on the joists. Do not nail the boards in place until you are satisfied with their arrangement and spacing. Install deck boards "bark side up." Pre-drill nail holes near the ends of boards to prevent splitting. Nail decking in place.

Deck Materials

Description	Quantity	Size	Length
Posts	6 pieces	4x4	varied
Skirtboard	2 pieces	2x12	10'
Skirtboard	2 pieces	2x12	8'
Ledgers	2 pieces	2x4	8'
Joists	4 pieces	2x8	8'
Deckboards	26 pieces	2x4	10'

Other Materials

1 lb. 16-penny nails
8 2x8 joist hangers
10 3/8" x 2-1/2" lag screws
10 3/8" x 6" carriage bolts, washers and nuts
6 Concrete footings with nailing blocks

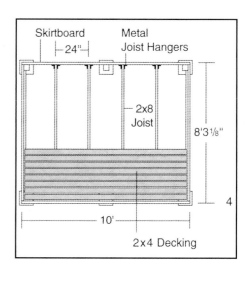

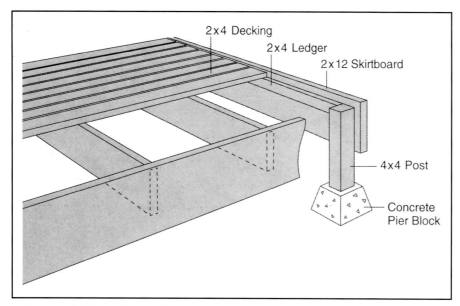

Courtesy of California Redwood Association

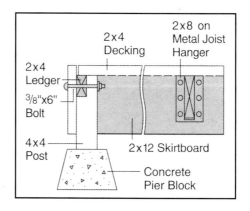

Deck Over Concrete

Courtesy of California Redwood Association

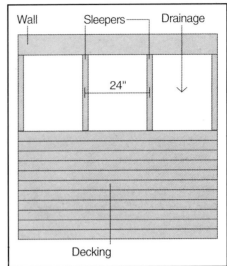

Wall   Sleepers   Drainage

24"

Decking

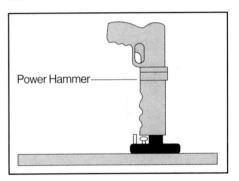

Power Hammer

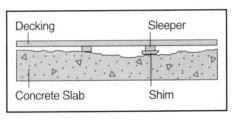

Decking   Sleeper

Concrete Slab   Shim

Building a deck over an existing concrete slab is an easy way to get the complete enjoyment of a deck at a fraction of the labor and cost, according to the California Redwood Association. Concrete slabs that have been around for years are often cracked, uneven, or just plain unsightly. Stable, weather-resistant redwood can cover all these defects beautifully.

There are two basic steps to converting your concrete slab to wood, attaching sleepers to the concrete slab and nailing 2x4 or 2x6 decking to the sleepers, as follows:

Sleepers. First lay the sleepers down in the spots where they will be attached. They should be spaced 24 inches on center. The sleepers may be random lengths because the concrete slab will support the full length of the sleeper. This can be a savings because short lengths are often less expensive. If the concrete slab is cracked or uneven, this is the time to level the sleepers with shims or small pieces of wood. If the concrete slab is adjacent to the wall of a house, sleepers should run perpendicular to the wall for best drainage.

The best way to attach sleepers to the concrete slab is with a "power hammer," which uses explosive charges to shoot special nails into concrete. Power hammers are available at building supply and tool rental centers. They are easy to use and are designed with safety features to help prevent accidents. Follow manufacturer's directions for safe operation.

Decking. The decking should be laid in place before nailing. Random lengths of Construction Common/Deck Common can be used for decking as long as butt joints meet over the sleepers. It is good practice not to have two butt joints adjacent to each other on the same sleeper. Install deck boards "bark side up."

Use stainless steel, aluminum or top quality, hot-dipped galvanized nails and fasteners for exterior projects. Other types of fasteners will corrode when exposed to moisture and will cause unsightly stains.

For 2" decking, use 10-penny nails. Decking nails should penetrate 1-1/2" into the sleepers. Pre-drill holes at the ends of boards to avoid splitting. To allow for water drainage, decking boards should be space about 1/8" apart.

Compact Deck

Here's an attractive deck design that two handy persons with intermediate building skills can build in a weekend, according to the Southern Pine Council.

This deck was designed by Deborah J. Ford, AIA, for a level site, assuring comfortable seating. Using the appropriate lumber, it can be set directly on the ground. However, local soil conditions may warrant the installation of 4x4 corner posts, set in concrete beneath the deck frame, to minimize the effects of ground subsidence over time. An easier alternative is to place concrete block footers at the deck frame's four corners. Ask a local builder if either support device is necessary.

Materials

Quantity	Size	Length	To Make
4	2x12	12'	Deck Framing (F1-F4)
5	2x12	10'	Deck Framing (J1-J5)
3	2x10	8'	12 Seat Supports (R)
6	2x6	12'	Deck Framing (F4,F5); Blocking
12	2x4	10'	Seat Frames, rail supports, ledgers
22	2x2	17"	Railing Spindles
372 lin.ft.	5/4x6 R.E.D.		D1 16 pcs. 8' D2 20 pcs. 10' (Deck, Seats & Back Rail) D3 4 pcs. 11' (Steps)

Other

Hot-dipped galvanized nails: 8d (approx. 8 lbs.) to fasten decking, steps, seat and rail, 12d (approx. 10 lbs.) to assemble deck framing

11 hot-dipped galvanized bolts, 5" x 3/16" , with 22 washers

Construction adhesive for treated wood

Water repellent sealer.

Instructions

1. Build the deck frame. From the 12' 2x12 lumber, cut members F1, F2, F3, and F4 according to the Deck Framing Plan. Assemble with 12d nails and construction adhesive.
2. Complete step frame, cutting F5 (10'-10") and F6 (10'-7-1/2") from 2x6 lumber. Attach to protruding ends of F1 and F2. Check for square. overall dimensions of deck frame should be 10'-11-1/2" by 10'-10-1/2".
3. Carefully measure the inside distance between F1 and F3; it should be 9'-10". Cut five 2x12 joists, J1 through J5 to fit between F1 and F3. Refer to section A-A for joist location. Attach to deck frame with 12d nails and construction adhesive. As each joist is installed, recheck for square.
4. From the remaining 2x6 lumber, cut blocking to attach at midpoints of all joists and between J1 and F2 and J5 and F4. Align top edge of blocking with top of 2x12 joist. Attach blocking adjacent to seat frame locations between

Courtesy of Southern Pine Council

F2 and J1. Attach blocking at steps, between F4 and F5, and between F3 and F6. Add diagonal blocking at four deck corners and at the intersection of the steps. Refer to Deck Framing Plan for all blocking locations.

5. Cut all 2x10 lumber into two-foot lengths, making a total of 12 vertical seat supports (R). From two 10' 2x4s, cut 15" ledger pieces (S), making a total of 12. From four more 2x4s, cut a total of 20 seat frame members (W), each 21" long. From the remaining six 2x4s, cut 12 rail supports (T) 3'-8-1/4" long, plus four 21" seat frame members (W). Refer to Section A-A for end-cutting details of parts T (both ends cut at 45°) and W (one end at 60°); use miter box to make uniform cuts.
6. Construct seat framing as shown in Sections A-A and C-C. Using 12d nails and adhesive, attach 2x4 rail supports (T) to F1 and F2 at locations shown in Deck Framing Plan. Attach 2x10 vertical (R) to 2x12 joists and frame and to 2x6 blocking with 12d nails and adhesive. Bottom of 2x10 should be 3" above ground level; vertically, the 2x10 is positioned 5-1/2" in from the outer edge of the deck frame. Note: Use a single piece of decking (5-1/2" wide) to aid positioning of 2x10 (R). Next, attach pairs of 2x4 seat supports (W) flush with top edge of 2x10 vertical (R).
7. Where the 2x4 seat supports (W) and rail support (T) intersect, drill a centered hole to receive 5x3/16" bolt with washers. Note: For optimum appearance, a 4-1/2" x 3/16" bolt can be used if countersunk 3/8" on both sides.
8. Precut and preposition all Radius Edge Decking (R.E.D.) before nailing in place. Note: Install all decking material "bark side up." For the deck platform's four sides, three pieces of

decking (D2) form a "picture frame" around 16 pieces decking (D1) cut to a length of approximately 7'-2"; take actual measurement before cutting the 8' lengths of decking. At seat frame locations, some notching of D2 decking will be required; a small hand (keyhole) or saber saw is helpful here. Use miter box to cut 45° decking & step joints at corners.

9. Once all R.E.D. pieces are in position, attach to deck frame with 8d nails and construction adhesive. The R.E.D. steps (D3) are completed in similar fashion. Decking on steps should overhang 1/2" beyond 2x6 framing (F5 and F6).

10. Attach R.E.D. seating to 2x4 frames (W) using 8d nails and adhesive. Miter ends where the two benches intersect.

Note: Do not nail R.E.D. seating into end of 2x10 (R). Attach R.E.D. rail to the top of 2x4 support (T) in similar fashion.

11. From 2x2 material, cut 22 railing spindles (V) 17" in overall length. The top should be cut to 45°; the bottom cut straight. Equally space two spindles between each 2x4 support (T). Use 8d nails and construction adhesive to attach each spindle to the back of R.E.D. rail and seating. Pre-drill all holes in spindles.

12. Construction is complete. Apply a water repellent sealer to all exposed wood surfaces. Properly dispose of treated lumber scraps. Note: Do not burn treated lumber.

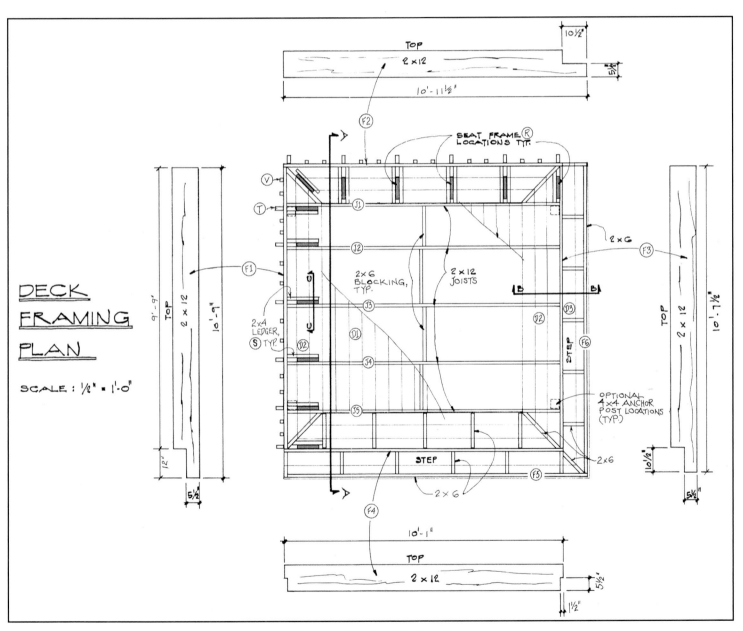

Courtesy of Southern Pine Council

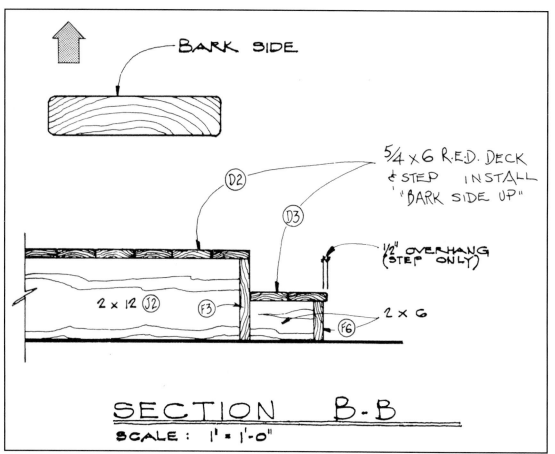

BARK SIDE

5/4 x 6 R.E.D. DECK & STEP INSTALL "BARK SIDE UP"

D2

D3

1/2" OVERHANG (STEP ONLY)

2 x 12 J2

F3

2 x 6

F6

SECTION B-B
SCALE : 1" = 1'-0"

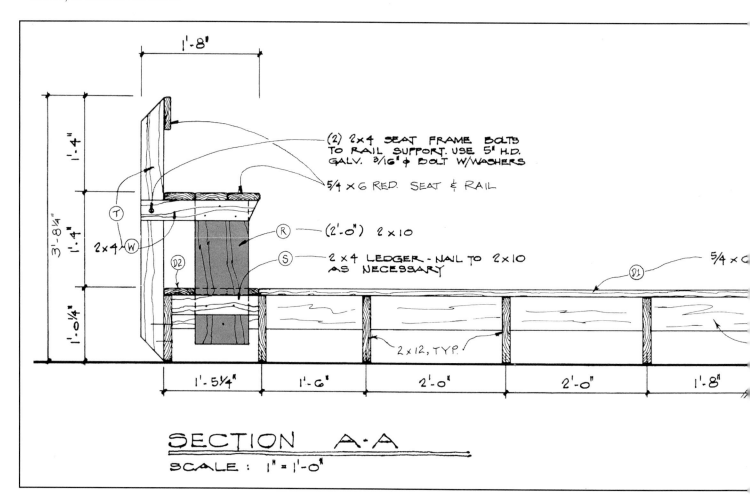

1'-8"

(2) 2x4 SEAT FRAME BOLTS TO RAIL SUPPORT. USE 5" H.D. GALV. 3/16" ⌀ BOLT W/WASHERS

5/4 x 6 RED. SEAT & RAIL

(2'-0") 2 x 10

2 x 4 LEDGER - NAIL TO 2 x 10 AS NECESSARY

T

W

2 x 4

D2

R

S

D1

5/4 x

3'-8¼"

1'-4"

1'-4"

1'-4"

1'-0¼"

2 x 12, TYP.

1'-5¼"   1'-6"   2'-0"   2'-0"   1'-8"

SECTION A·A
SCALE : 1" = 1'-0"

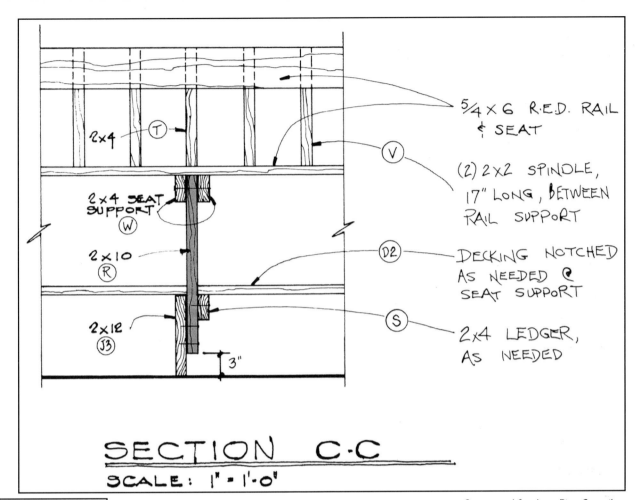

2x4 (T)

2x4 SEAT
SUPPORT
(W)

2x10
(R)

2x12
(J3)

3"

⁵⁄₄ × 6 R.E.D. RAIL
& SEAT

(2) 2x2 SPINDLE,
17" LONG, BETWEEN
RAIL SUPPORT

DECKING NOTCHED
AS NEEDED @
SEAT SUPPORT

2x4 LEDGER,
AS NEEDED

(V)

(D2)

(S)

SECTION C·C
SCALE: 1" = 1'·0"

Courtesy of Southern Pine Council

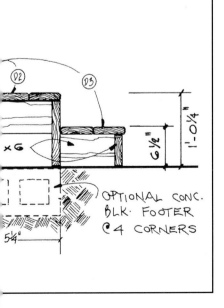

OPTIONAL CONC.
BLK· FOOTER
@ 4 CORNERS

6½"

1'·0¼"

5¼"

×6

(D2)   (D3)

Bilevel Deck with Sunscreen

Courtesy of Southern Pine Council

6	2x10	12'
3	2x10	14'
2	2x6	20'
1	2x12	10'
78	5/4x6	14'
14	R.E.D.	12'
30	R.E.D.	10'
3	4x8	1/2" Ext. Plywood
3	4x8	Lattice

Other
20 lbs.   of 16d common nails
10 lbs.   10d common nails
10 lbs.   10d ring shank nails
10 lbs.   10d finishing nails
5 lbs. of joist hangers
100 1/4"x3-1/2" lag screws, with 1/4" washers
14 1/2"x6" lag screws
56 1/2" washers
38 single 2x6 joist hangers
6-10 mil polyethylene, for planter liner, approx. 12sq.yds.
Concrete for setting posts.
Vegetation barrier (beneath deck): either gravel or 6 mil poly film.
20 to 30 pieces to brace post while concrete sets, can be 1x2, 1x4 or 2x4, in lengths of 6' to 8'.

Naturally versatile, a deck can be a breakfast room on sunny mornings, a play area for children, a sitting room for reading, a kitchen for cookouts, or a living room for garden parties.

This plan from the Southern Pine Council, as shown, is intended for a level site, with the lower deck level adjoining an existing house or other building. Design modifications can be made to suit a sloping or uneven site. Consider elevating the sunscreen section (rear of deck) over down-sloping terrain, creating convenient storage beneath the deck. This under-deck storage area can easily be enclosed with prefabricated lattice panels. Depending on your particular site, the locations for planters can be altered, as well.

Additional seating can be provided with simple benches along the perimeter of the lower deck level. Anchor cutoffs from the 6x6 posts to support a 2x4 bench platform/frame. Use 3 lengths of 5/4"x6" Radius Edge Decking for the bench seat.

This project requires advanced carpentry skills and at least two people to build. You may want to enlist the services of a local builder; contact your Home Builders Association for referrals.

When it's complete, invite the neighbors over, relax, and enjoy your new outdoor living space.

Materials

Quantity	Material	Length
8	6x6	14'
6	6x6	8'
14	2x2	8'
26	2x6	14'
14	2x6	12'
12	2x6	14'
16	2x4	12'

Instructions

1. Determine exact location of deck. Consider the bench and sunscreen position in relation to the sun. It can be built over an existing patio or be placed on a level grade. To prevent vegetation growth beneath deck, cover area with poly film or 1" gravel layer. Locate post positions according to the plan. Be sure you are clear of underground utility service lines. Dig 18" diameter post holes at least 32" deep, and allow for 6" concrete to be poured on all sides and below each post. Check with a local builder to see if soil conditions warrant deeper post placement.

2. Cut eight 6x6 posts to 12' 6", for locations A through H. Chamfer top 1/2" as shown. Place 2' 2" below ground. See Detail 5. Use stakes, line, and level to keep posts square and vertical. Use 2x4 studs to erect bracing while concrete sets. Leave nail heads exposed for easy removal.

3. Cut 8' 6x6 posts to 7' (or set 1' deeper), for all other post locations. Set in concrete and brace as needed. Allow time for concrete to set, according to supplier's recommendations. Do not set posts in freezing weather.

4. Build 2x6 lower deck framing while concrete sets. Trim six 12' 2x6s to 11' 11-1/4" for center joists; arrange 24" on center, according to plan. Attach 14' 2x6 ledger across

ends, using 16d nails and construction adhesive.

5. Attach 2x6 ledger to house using pairs of 1/2"x6" lag screws and washers 24" on center, as shown in Detail 4. Add four 1/2" washers to each screw for spacer between ledger and siding/sheathing. All lower deck framing members should be pressure treated for ground contact application (.40).

6. Reinforce joists with 2x6 bridging 24" on center. Use 16d nails and adhesive on all joints. Make periodic checks for level and square. Toe-nail joists to posts J, K, and M.

7. Begin structural support for upper deck. Attach 2x10 blocking to 6x6 posts to support 2x10 beams. See Detail 7. Use three 1/4"x3-1/2" lag screws, washers, and liberal adhesive per blocking locations. Countersink screws 1/2" at post K only. Note that all perimeter 2x10 beams are 1" higher on posts than center beams, so that they finish flush with 1" decking. See Detail 6. Therefore, to have finished deck surface at 1' 8" above grade, 2x10 blocks at posts A, E, I, J, K, M, L, H, N, and D will be positioned 1-1/2" above grade level. See Detail 7. Blocking at center posts B, C, F, and G will extend to 1/2" above grade. Use chalk line and level to aid alignment of blocking.

8. Attach one 14' 2x10 to posts J, K, and M atop blocking. Attach another to posts F and B. Fasten as in Step 7.

9. Install double 2x10 space between posts K and L. Add additional 2x10 block to post K for ledger. Similarly, install double 2x10s between L and M. Complete planter support beams by adding a 2x10 to inside of span installed in Step 8 between K and M.

10. Install remaining perimeter 2x10 beams, one each connecting A-I, L-H, and H-D. Secure to posts E and N, as well.

11. Attach remaining 14' 2x10 to posts C and G, intersecting with double 2x10 span between K and L at planter. Toe-nail to planter beam.

12. Attach 2x4 ledger to both sides of 2x10 beam spanning between K and L, and to the inside of double 2x10 beam between M and L. Refer to plan and Detail 3. Add 4' 2x4 ledger, centered on joist locations, at beam between I and J. Refer to Detail 6. Use 10d nails and liberal adhesive to fasten all ledgers.

13. Mark 2x10 beams for 2x6 joist locations using chalk line, 24" on center. Refer to plan and Detail 5 for joist locations beneath bench at rear.

14. Fasten 2x6 joist hangers to 2x10 beams at joist locations using joist hanger nails.

15. Cut 2x6 joists from 14' lengths. Install joists in hangers, securing in place with joist hanger nails.

16. Add 2x6 bridging 24" on center, between all joists. Attach with 16d nails and adhesive. All joists and bridging should rest 1" below finished deck level.

17. Using 2x6 blocks, enclose posts F and G on the two sides without a joist or beam. Use 16d nails and adhesive.

18. Install 2x6 joists inside planter 16" on center, resting on 2x4 ledger. See Detail 5. Upper deck framing is complete.

19. Install lower decking. Arrange 14' lengths of (R.E.D.) across lower deck framing. Fasten bark side up using 10d ring shank nails and adhesive. Attach 2x4 edge flush with decking surface, securing it to end of 2x6 beams with 10d nails and adhesive. See Detail 2.

20. Build step to upper level. Cut five 2x6 blocks, 9" long. Measure exact distance between posts J and K and cut 2x6 cap to this length. Attach two blocks to ends of this 2x6; space other three blocks equally, approximately 21" on center. Refer to plan and Detail 1. Toe-nail frame to 2x10 beam and nail end blocks to posts J and K using 16d nails. Attach R.E.D. decking to frame with 10d ring shank nails and adhesive.

21. Install upper level R.E.D. material, as in Step 19. Decking extends beneath planter location. For angled ends, snap a chalk line across R.E.D. ends between posts I and J, and H and L.

    Attach 2x4 edge trim to 2x10 beam between posts L and M, with top edge of 2x4 flush with R.E.D. surface; use 10d nails and adhesive. See Detail 3.

22. With 2x4 material, build 35" stud wall for 3 sides of planter. Studs should be 16" on center. Miter top and bottom 2x4 chords as needed. Build walls with 10d nails and adhesive. Cut and attach 1/2" plywood to inside face of all 3 walls; use 10d nails. Secure bottom 2x4 chord to 2x10 beams using 16d nails and adhesive. Refer to Detail 3.

    From 10' R.E.D. material cut 35" pieces for vertical planter sides. Cap planter with R.E.D. pieces, miter joints, and attach to 2x4 top chord. Attach all R.E.D. material to planter with 10d finishing nails and adhesive.

23. Install planter liner. Cut poly film as needed to cover interior of planter. Tack or staple to plywood wall.

24. Complete railing. Attach 2x6 rail to posts, with top edge 36" above deck surface. Rail extends between posts A and I, I and J, L and H, and N and D. Attach to posts with 16d nails and adhesive. From 2x2 material, cut 28 rail spindles 42" long; miter ends at 45 degrees. Attach to posts with 16d nails and adhesive. (Note: model deck used spindles 4" on center, according to builder's preference.)

25. Install sunscreen frame. Snap a chalk line down the center of two 20' 2x6s. Start 8" from one end and mark every 5". These marks aid positioning of louvers. Measure exact distance between 6x6 posts and build 2x6 sunscreen frame to fit area outlined by posts A, D, E and H.

    Put sides of marked 2x6s to the inside of frame. Tack 2x6 blocks 6" from the top inside faces of 6x6 posts for temporary support of 2x6 frame. Using ladders and helpers, lift frame into place and attach to posts with 16d nails.

26. Cut louvers. Measure exact span between 20' 2x6s and cut R.E.D. louvers to fit. Tilt louvers at 45 degrees angle against the sun. See louver location detail. Attach to frame using 10d finishing nails.

27. Build seat frames. Make 13 seat frames using two 2x6 vertical supports and one 2x4 seat support. Refer to Detail 5. Build with 10d nails and adhesive. Refer to plan for seat frame locations. Trim back supports of end frames attached

to posts A and D, to fit beneath 2x6 railing. Position pairs of frames at posts B and C, plus two frames equally space between posts A and B, B and C, and C and D. Position last frame at mid-point of span between B and C. Completed frames sit atop R.E.D. decking. Attach frames to posts and/or toe-nail to deck joists as needed; use 16d nails.

28. Install R.E.D. seating. Using 10' R.E.D. material, attach seating to frames, three pieces each to form back, seat, and front. Add cap across seat frame tops, cutting pieces to fit between rear posts. Use 10d finishing nail and adhesive to attach all R.E.D. material. Install bark side up.

29. Build side steps. Cut 3 stringers from 2x12. Refer to Detail 8. Attach one each to inside face of posts D and H, using lag screws with washers. Measure exact distance between these end stringers and cut 2x4 ledger to fit between them; attach 20 2x10 perimeter beam with 10d nails and adhesive. Notch remaining 2x12 stringer to fit ledger; toe-nail to 2x10 using 16d nails. Cut 6 R.E.D. pieces to form treads and caps as shown; attach to stringers using 10d nails and adhesive.

30. Install lattice panels. Cut sections to fit inside openings below upper deck level between posts A and E, E and I, and J, L and H, and N and D. Attach to 2x10 beams using joist hanger nails and adhesive (Builder's option: trim out lattice panels with 2x2 material.)

31. Construction is complete. Apply a water repellent sealer to all exposed wood surfaces, according to manufacturer's instructions.

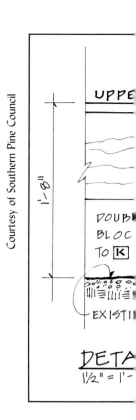

UPPE

DOUB
BLOC
TO K

EXISTI

DETA
1/2" = 1'-

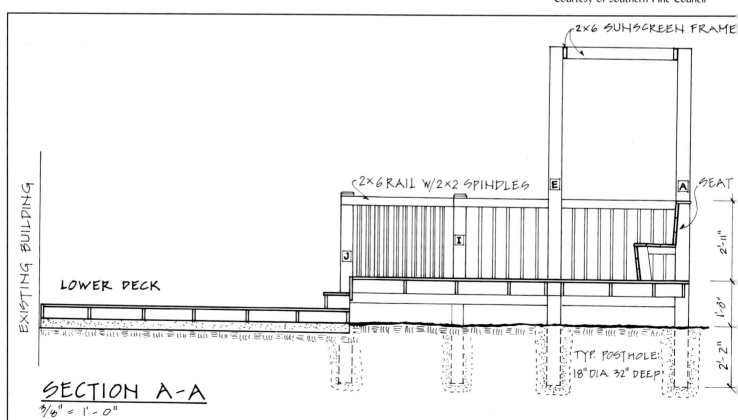

2x6 SUNSCREEN FRAME

2x6 RAIL W/2x2 SPINDLES

SEAT

EXISTING BUILDING

LOWER DECK

TYP. POSTHOLE:
18" DIA. 32" DEEP

SECTION A-A
3/8" = 1'-0"

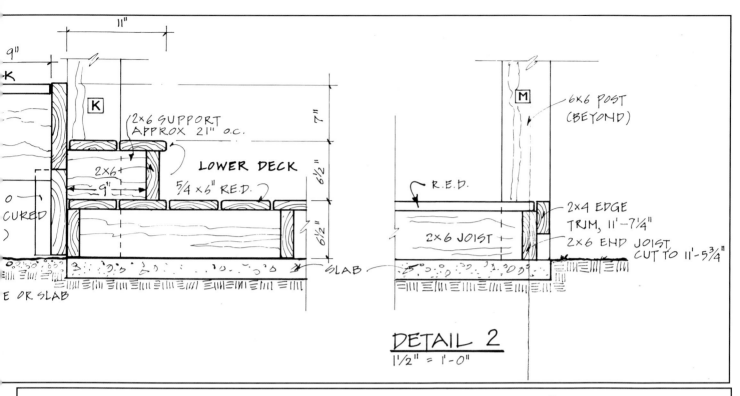

9"

11"

K

K

2×6 SUPPORT
APPROX 21" o.c.

7"

LOWER DECK

5/4 ×6" R.E.D.

6½"

2×6+

9"

6½"

O
CURED
)

E OR SLAB

SLAB

M

6×6 POST
(BEYOND)

R.E.D.

2×6 JOIST

2×4 EDGE
TRIM, 11'-7¼"

2×6 END JOIST
CUT TO 11'-5¾"

DETAIL 2
1½" = 1'-0"

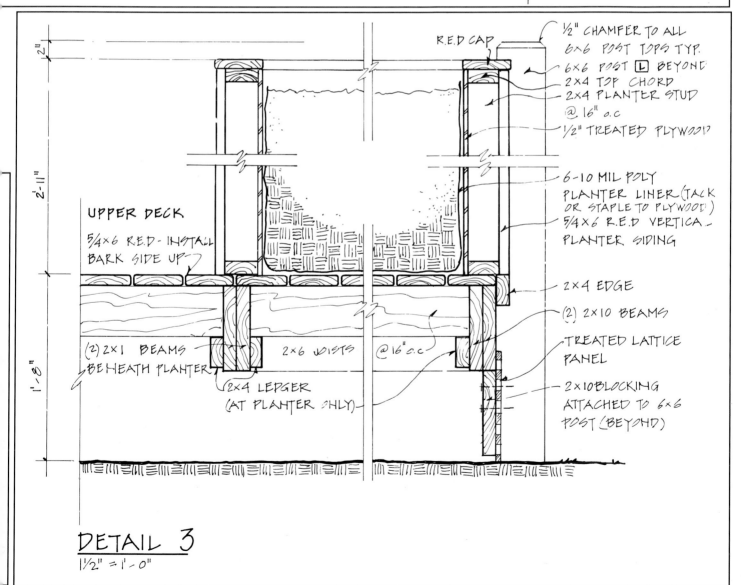

R.E.D CAP

½" CHAMFER TO ALL
6×6 POST TOPS TYP.

6×6 POST L BEYOND

2×4 TOP CHORD

2×4 PLANTER STUD
@ 16" o.c

½" TREATED PLYWOOD

6-10 MIL POLY
PLANTER LINER (TACK
OR STAPLE TO PLYWOOD)

5/4×6 R.E.D VERTICAL
PLANTER SIDING

2"

2'-11"

UPPER DECK

5/4×6 R.E.D - INSTALL
BARK SIDE UP

(2) 2×1 BEAMS
BENEATH PLANTER

2×6 JOISTS

@16" o.c

2×4 LEDGER
(AT PLANTER ONLY)

1'-8"

2×4 EDGE

(2) 2×10 BEAMS

TREATED LATTICE
PANEL

2×10 BLOCKING
ATTACHED TO 6×6
POST (BEYOND)

DETAIL 3
1½" = 1'-0"

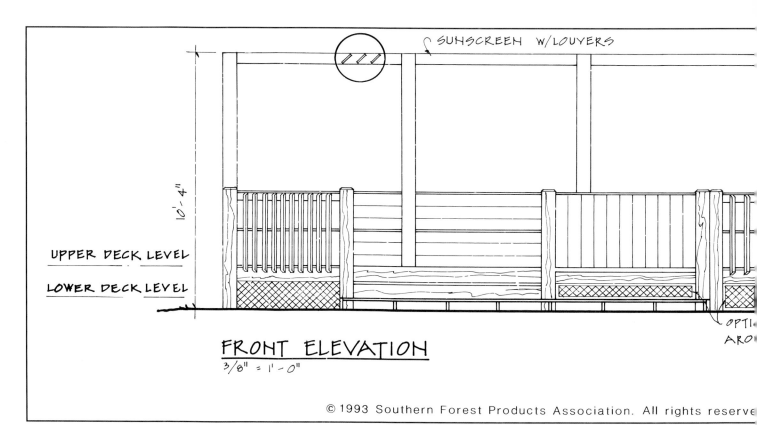

SUNSCREEN W/LOUVERS

10'-4"

UPPER DECK LEVEL

LOWER DECK LEVEL

OPTI
ARO

FRONT ELEVATION
3/8" = 1'-0"

Courtesy of Southern Pine Council

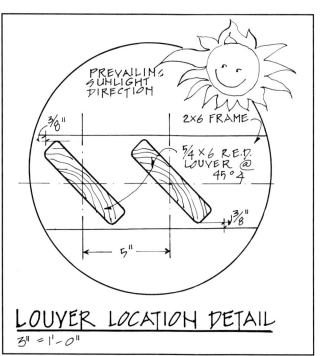

PREVAILING SUNLIGHT DIRECTION

2x6 FRAME

3/8"

5/4 X 6 R.E.D. LOUVER @ 45°

3/8"

5"

LOUVER LOCATION DETAIL
3" = 1'-0"

× 2 TRIM
TICE PANELS

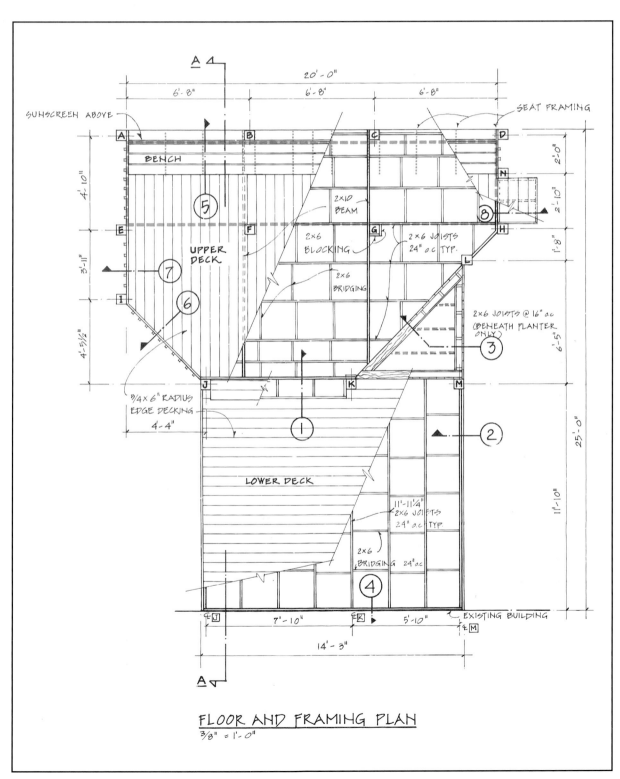

FLOOR AND FRAMING PLAN
3/8" = 1'-0"

Text within the plan:

A
20'-0"
6'-8"   6'-8"   6'-8"
SUNSCREEN ABOVE
SEAT FRAMING
A   B   C   D
BENCH
N
4'-10"
2'-0"
5   2×10 BEAM
2'-0"
E   F   G   H
2×6 BLOCKING
2×6 JOISTS 24" o.c TYP.
8
3'-11"
7   2×6 BRIDGING
L
I
6   2×6 JOISTS @ 16" o.c (BENEATH PLANTER ONLY)
4'-5½"
3
6'-5"
J   K   M
1'-8"
3/4×6" RADIUS EDGE DECKING
4'-4"
1   2
25'-0"
LOWER DECK
11'-11¼" 2×6 JOISTS 24" o.c TYP.
2×6 BRIDGING 24"o.c
4
11'-10"
₵ J   ₵ K   ₵ M
EXISTING BUILDING
7'-10"   5'-10"
14'-3"
A

97

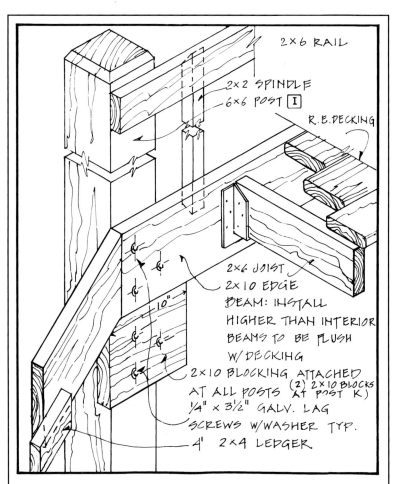

2×6 RAIL

2×2 SPINDLE

6×6 POST ⬛I

R.E.DECKING

2×6 JOIST

2×10 EDGE BEAM: INSTALL HIGHER THAN INTERIOR BEAMS TO BE FLUSH W/DECKING

2×10 BLOCKING ATTACHED AT ALL POSTS (2) 2×10 BLOCKS AT POST K)

¼" × 3½" GALV. LAG SCREWS W/WASHER TYP.

4' 2×4 LEDGER

10"

DETAIL 6
HO SCALE

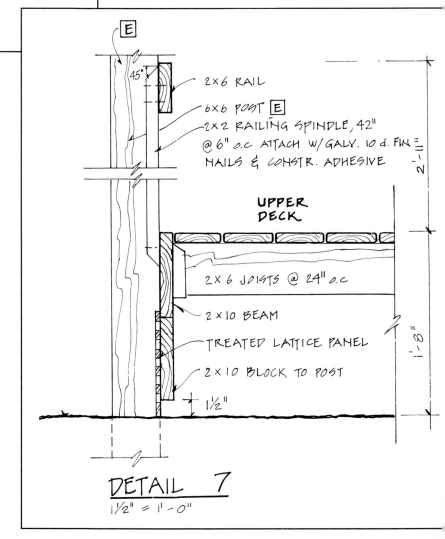

⬛E

45°

2×6 RAIL

6×6 POST ⬛E

2×2 RAILING SPINDLE, 42" @ 6" o.c. ATTACH W/GALV. 10 d. FIN NAILS & CONSTR. ADHESIVE

UPPER DECK

2×6 JOISTS @ 24" o.c.

2×10 BEAM

TREATED LATTICE PANEL

2×10 BLOCK TO POST

1½"

2'-11"

1'-8"

DETAIL 7
1½" = 1'-0"

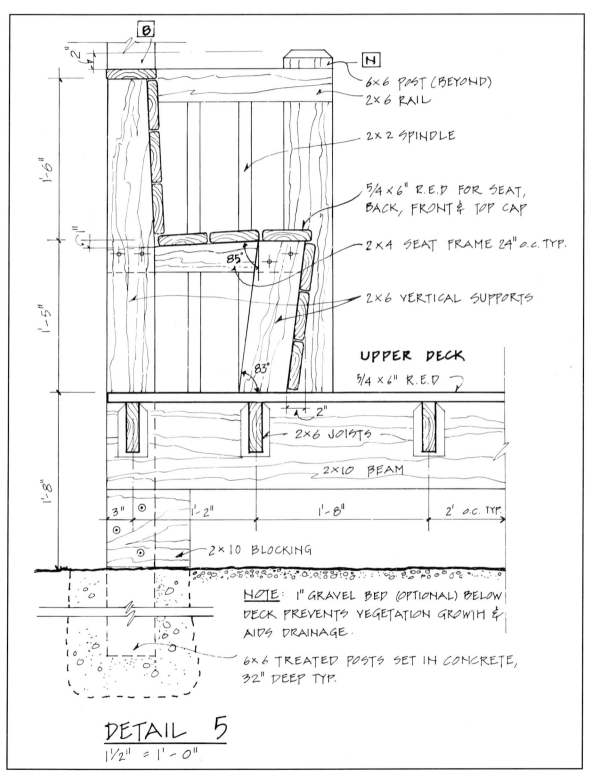

2"

B

N

6×6 POST (BEYOND)
2×6 RAIL

2×2 SPINDLE

5/4×6" R.E.D FOR SEAT,
BACK, FRONT & TOP CAP

1'-6"

1"

85°

2×4 SEAT FRAME 24" o.c. TYP.

2×6 VERTICAL SUPPORTS

1'-5"

UPPER DECK
5/4 × 6" R.E.D

83°

2"

1'-8"

2×6 JOISTS

2×10 BEAM

3"   1'-2"   1'-8"   2' o.c. TYP.

2×10 BLOCKING

NOTE: 1" GRAVEL BED (OPTIONAL) BELOW
DECK PREVENTS VEGETATION GROWTH &
AIDS DRAINAGE.

6×6 TREATED POSTS SET IN CONCRETE,
32" DEEP TYP.

DETAIL 5
1 1/2" = 1'-0"

Courtesy of Southern Pine Council

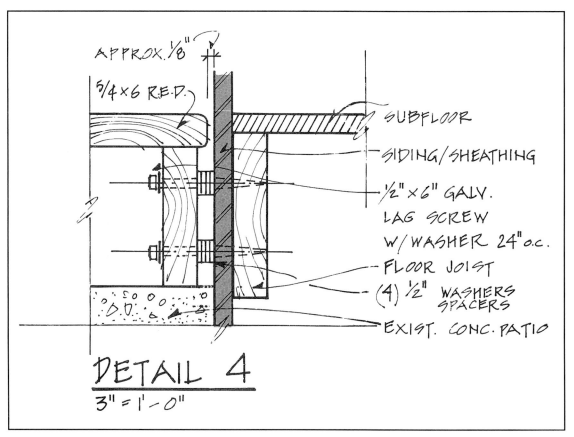

APPROX. 1/8"

5/4 × 6 R.E.D.

SUBFLOOR

SIDING/SHEATHING

1/2" × 6" GALV.
LAG SCREW
W/ WASHER 24" o.c.

FLOOR JOIST

(4) 1/2" WASHERS
SPACERS

EXIST. CONC. PATIO

DETAIL 4
3" = 1'-0"

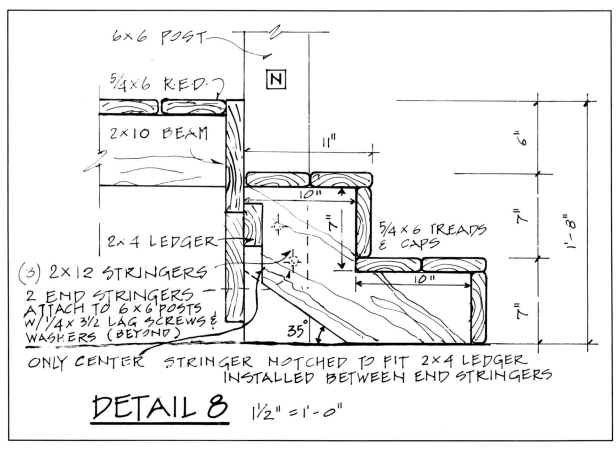

6×6 POST

5/4 × 6 R.E.D.

N

2×10 BEAM

11"

6"

10"

7"

5/4 × 6 TREADS
& CAPS

7"

1'-8"

2×4 LEDGER

(3) 2×12 STRINGERS

10"

2 END STRINGERS
ATTACH TO 6×6 POSTS
W/ 1/4 × 3 1/2 LAG SCREWS &
WASHERS (BEYOND)

35°

7"

ONLY CENTER STRINGER NOTCHED TO FIT 2×4 LEDGER
INSTALLED BETWEEN END STRINGERS

DETAIL 8   1 1/2" = 1'-0"

Ground-Level Deck

Decks work wonders in many different ways ... contemporary in style, yet simple and natural. They blend home and landscape with broad, inviting vistas creating a feeling of freedom and expansiveness, and offering an oasis of comfort in the open air. Sometimes the best room of the house is outside on the treated wood deck.

Naturally versatile, a deck can be a breakfast room on sunny mornings, a play area for children, a sitting room for reading, a kitchen for cookouts, or a living room for garden parties.

This ground-level deck plan designed by Glenn C. Higgins, AIA, for the Southern Pine Council will take you step by step through the construction process. The design uses Southern Pine radius edge decking in a parquet configuration for a great-looking addition to your outdoor living space.

Courtesy of Southern Pine Council

Materials

Number of Pieces	Material	Length
4	2x8	20'
4	2x4	20'
2	2x8	12'
2	2x8	10'
32	2x6	10'
8	2x2	10'
84	1x6	10'

8d, 10d & 12d hot-dipped galvanized nails
40-1/4" x 3" hot-dipped galvanized lag screws
21-concrete blocks, 4" x 8" x 16"
Concrete or gravel for footings
Construction adhesive for pressure treated lumber
Water repellent sealer

Instructions

1. Determine exact location of the deck. On the sides that will adjoin your house or other building, omit 2x4 trim pieces.
2. Choose one of the footing options for support of the concrete blocks. Refer to plan for footing locations; the top of the blocks should be at ground level. Use stakes, line, and level to aid positioning of footings and blocks.
3. Build perimeter deck frame by cutting two 2x8s to 19' 6" and two more to 19' 3". Make a square frame using 12d nails and construction adhesive.
4. Install center support using two 12' 2x8s overlapping them at the center. Position them along the centerline of the deck frame. Use 10d nails and construction adhesive to nail the overlapping sections together and to attach this center support to the deck frame.
5. Complete the basic support frame by cutting two 2x8s to fit between the deck frame and the center support. Use 10d nails and construction adhesive to attach them to the deck frame along the centerline. Use 12d nails to toe-nail these members to the overlapping 2x8 sections of the center support. Make sure entire deck frame assembly remains square.
6. Determine the deck board direction for your parquet pattern in each of the four quadrants.
7. Attach 2x2 ledgers to the 2x8 deck frame and center supports. Ledgers support both ends of the 2x6 joists. Be sure combined ledger and 2x6 joist height is flush with top of 2x8s. Attach ledger to 2x8s using construction adhesive and the galvanized lag screws. Use 5 screws per ledger, spacing them about 18" apart. Predrill 3/16" holes to receive lag screws.
8. Install 2x6 joists 16" on center perpendicular to deck board direction in each quadrant. Use 10d nails. Refer to plan for exact joist positioning. Check for square.
9. Along the centerline of each quadrant, install 2x6 bridging between the joists. Stagger their placement to aid nailing: use 10d nails. Tops of bridging and joists should be flush.
10. Begin arranging 10' 1x6 deck boards. Start at the center of the deck and build the parquet pattern out to each edge, allowing the board length to hang over the 2x8 perimeter deck frame.
11. Attach deck boards to frame and joists using 8d nails and construction adhesive. Be sure deck boards are "bark side up." When nailing near the end of the boards, remember to either blunt nail points or predrill holes to avoid splitting.

12. When all 21 deck boards per quadrant have been attached, evenly cut all the ends flush with the 2x8 perimeter frame.
13. Attach the 2x4 trim pieces to the 2x8 frame using 10d nails. The top edge of the 2x4 trim should align with the deck board's surface.
14. Construction is complete. Apply a coat of water repellent sealer to all exposed surfaces.

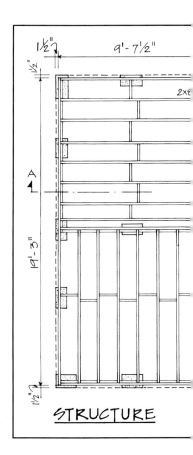

STRUCTURE

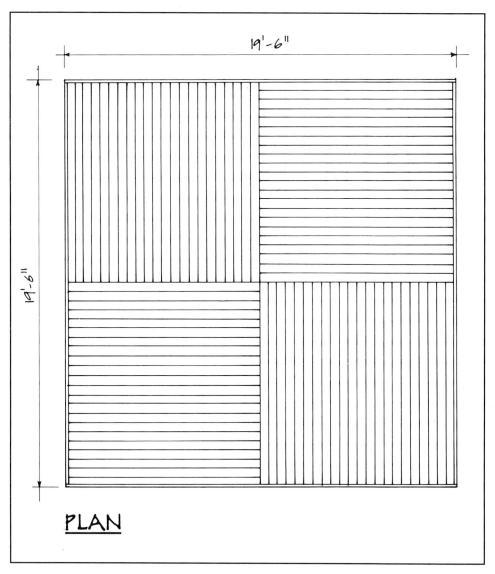

PLAN

Courtesy of Southern Pine Council

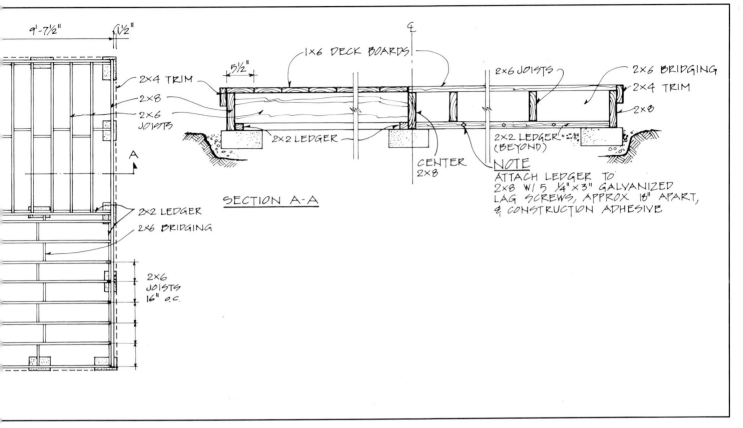

9'-7½"   1½"

2×4 TRIM
2×8
2×6 JOISTS

1×6 DECK BOARDS   2×6 JOISTS   2×6 BRIDGING
5½"   2×4 TRIM
                                   2×8

2×2 LEDGER   CENTER   2×2 LEDGER (BEYOND)
              2×8

A

SECTION A-A

NOTE
ATTACH LEDGER TO 2×8 W/ 5 ¼"×3" GALVANIZED LAG SCREWS, APPROX 18" APART, & CONSTRUCTION ADHESIVE

2×2 LEDGER
2×6 BRIDGING

2×6 JOISTS 16" o.c.

Courtesy of Southern Pine Counci

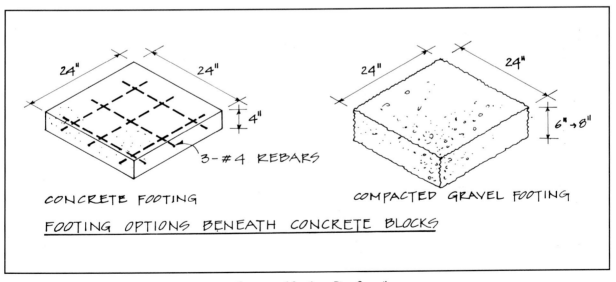

24"   24"
                    4"

3-#4 REBARS

CONCRETE FOOTING

24"   24"
                    6"→8"

COMPACTED GRAVEL FOOTING

FOOTING OPTIONS BENEATH CONCRETE BLOCKS

Courtesy of Southern Pine Council

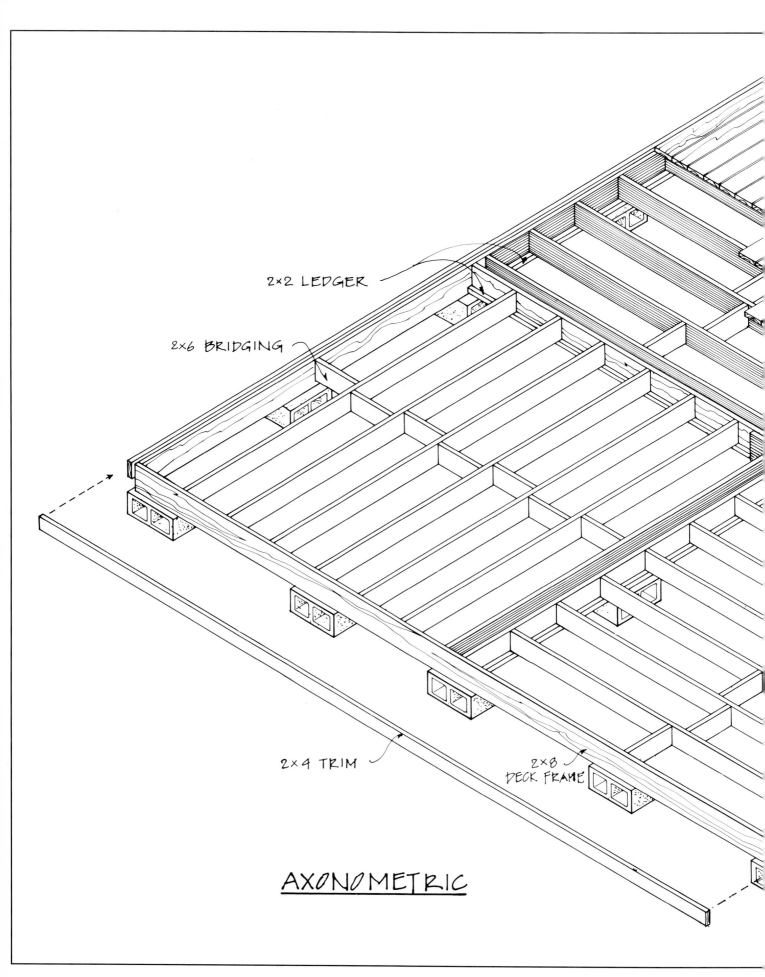

2×2 LEDGER

2×6 BRIDGING

2×4 TRIM

2×8
DECK FRAME

AXONOMETRIC

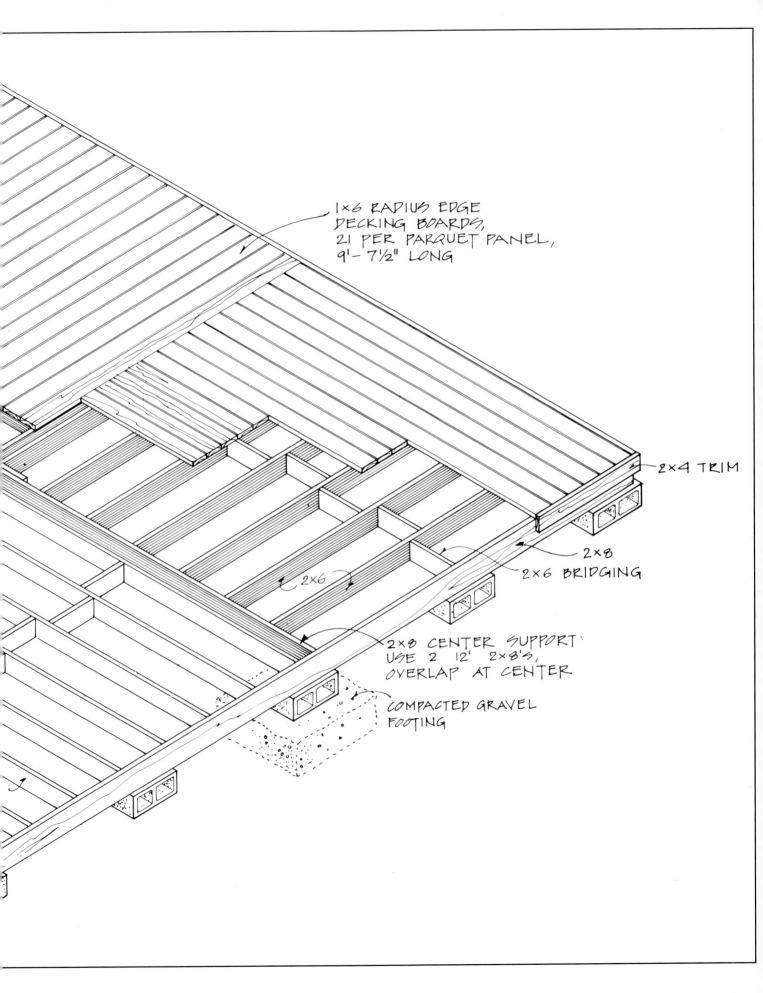

1×6 RADIUS EDGE
DECKING BOARDS,
21 PER PARQUET PANEL,
9'- 7½" LONG

2×4 TRIM

2×8

2×6 BRIDGING

2×6

2×8 CENTER SUPPORT
USE 2 12' 2×8'S,
OVERLAP AT CENTER

COMPACTED GRAVEL
FOOTING

Deck with Steps

Often, home and property don't occupy the same level ground. So any attempts to add-on outdoor living space call for elevating the new addition. An elevated deck is the perfect choice for such a project. This deck design from the Southern Pine Council can easily be tailored to suit your needs.

Naturally versatile, a deck can be a breakfast room on sunny mornings, a play area for children, a sitting room for reading, a kitchen for cookouts, or a living room for garden parties.

This deck plan designed by: Glenn C. Higgins, AIA, will take you step-by-step through the construction process.

Materials
Wood

# of Pieces	Material	Length
3	2x12s	8'
2	2x10s	12'
3	2x10s	10'
4	2x8s	12'
9	2x8s	12'
3	2x6s	12'
1	2x6	10'
1	2x6	14'
7	4x4s	10'
3	4x4s	8'
62	2x2s	8'
22	1x6s	12'
7	1x6s	10'

8d, 10d, & 12d hot-dipped galvanized nails
30 1/4"x4" hot-dipped galvanized lag screws
Hot-dipped galvanized bolts with nuts and washers: 15 1/2"x6", 6 1/2"x8"
Concrete for setting posts
Water repellent sealer
Construction adhesive for pressure treated lumber.

Instructions

1. Determine exact location and height of the deck and steps. Locate 4x4 post positions and dig holes for setting them in concrete as directed on the plan. Use stakes, line and level to aid positioning of posts. Use 8' 4x4 posts at end of stairs and where posts do not extend above deck surface. Allow sufficient time for concrete to set; follow recommendations of concrete mix manufacturer.
2. Determine location of finished deck surface (top of 1x6 deck boards) and mark all deck and stair corner posts. Use the line and level to help you establish this reference mark.
3. Trim the intermediate 4x4 posts to 1" below the reference mark on the corner posts.
4. Attach 12' 2x8 deck beams to 4x4 posts. Through-bolt beams to posts using three 1/2"x6" bolts per post. Countersink these, using 7/8" bit, 3/8" deep into 4x4 posts,

then drill through with 1/2" bit. Bottom edge of 2x8 beam should be 15-1/2" below the reference mark you made in Step 2. Refer to plan.
5. From the 8' 2x8, cut two beams to 3'-8-1/2". Attach to 4x4 posts beneath stair platform. Where platform adjoins deck, through-bolt this beam and the deck beam to 4x4 posts using the 8" bolts. Attach the other stair platform beam to 4x4 posts, using three 1/2"x6" bolts (countersink) at two locations. Refer to plan. Check for level and square.
6. Install 2x8 floor joists. From the 10' material, cut two end joists to 9' 2" to fit between 4x4 posts. Using 12d nails, toe-nail to posts making sure outside face of joist is flush with outside edge of 4x4 post.
7. Cut six 10' 2x8s to 9' 9". Arrange 16" on center from the end of the deck opposite the stair platform. Toe-nail to 2x8 beam using 12d nails.
8. Cut the two 14' 2x8s to 13' 0-1/4". These members span the deck and stair platform, 16" on center. Toe-nail to 2x8 beams using 12d nails.
9. From a 12' 2x8, cut two end joists for the stair platform, each 2' 11-3/4" long. Toe-nail one to 4x4 posts at the top of the stairs and the other flush with the outside of the deck. Refer to plan. Cut one piece to 3' 7" and attach to 4x4 posts just opposite the one at the head of the stairs; use 12d nails.
10. From the last 12' 2x8, cut bridging to brace joists along the deck's centerline. End nail joists to bridging using 10d nails.
11. Using scrap 2x8 material, make cleats for deck board sup-

port. Attach to 4x4 posts using 10d nails at locations noted on the plan.

12. Install decking. Start by attaching a 10' 2x10 fascia member to one end of the deck. The top edge should extend 1" above the 2x8 joist. Use 12d nails and construction adhesive to attach fascia to posts. Arrange 22 12' deck boards across 2x8 joists. Notch boards to fit around 4x4 posts. Be sure deck boards are installed "bark side up." Attach deck boards to floor joists using 8d nails and construction adhesive. Trim ends that extend beyond the 4x4 post's outer edge.

13. Repeat the procedure to install the stair platform decking. Start at the end facing the stairs. Use 10' deck material; cut three equal lengths from each. Once platform is in place, evenly trim the ends flush with outside edge of 4x4 posts.

14. Complete installation of 2x10 fascia around the deck's perimeter. Use 10d nails and construction adhesive. Top edge of 2x10 should be flush with top of deck boards.

15. Install 2x6 top rails. Chamfer the top edges as shown in the plan. Attach to 4x4 posts using two 4" lag screws and construction adhesive at each location. Pre-drill holes using 3/16" bit.

16. From the remaining 12' 2x6, cut a top rail for the stair banister. Chamfer and attach as directed in Step 15. Also from this material, cut a ledger to support stair stringers.

17. Build the stairs. Refer to plan for details on cutting stringers from 2x12 material. Mark one leg of your square at 6" and the other leg at 11". Outline the riser and tread as you slide the marked square along one edge of the 2x12, keeping both marks aligned with the edge. Once you have cut

one stringer, use it as a pattern for the other two. Notch should measure 1-1/2"x4". Hold one stringer in place and mark location of ledger's top edge on 4x4 post. Attach ledger to post using 12d nails and construction adhesive.

18. Toe-nail stringers to ledger and stair platform, using 12d nails. From the remaining 10' 1x6 deck boards, cut stair treads as indicated on the plan. Attach these to stringers using 8d nails and construction adhesive. Notch bottom tread board to fit around 4x4 post. Add 2x10 fascia to outside of stairs, using 10d nails.

19. Prepare 2x2 railing spindles. Each spindle is 3' 6" long with a 45-degree cut on the ends. Use miter box to cut ends. See detail on plan. Attach spindles 5" on center on stairs and all sides of the deck where a complete railing enclosure is desired. Use two 10d nails and construction adhesive at each end. Tack a line 2" below top edge of railing to aid the even placement of spindle tops.

20. Construction is complete. Apply a coat of water repellent sealer to all exposed surfaces.

Construction Note:

This design calls for 4x4 posts to support the deck, with the deck's surface approximately four feet above the grade. Use longer 4x4 posts for deck surface elevations of up to six feet above grade. For deck elevations from six to eight feet, use 4x6 posts.

Also, the materials list calls for a railing on all four sides of the deck. Ideally, one side of the deck will adjoin your house or other building; the railing can be omitted on this side, or trimmed to allow for a door opening.

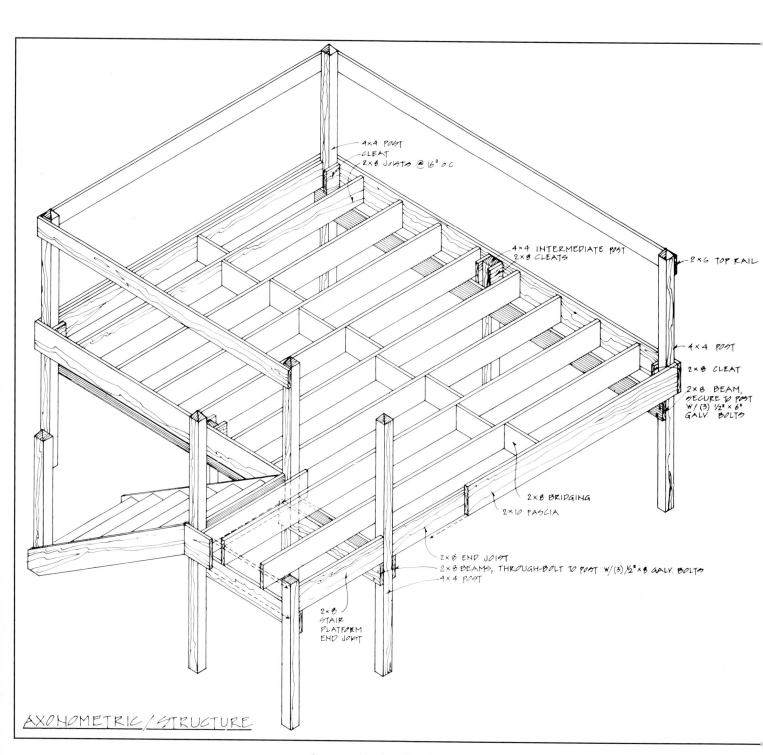

4×4 POST
CLEAT
2×8 JOISTS @ 16" O.C

4×4 INTERMEDIATE POST
2×8 CLEATS

2×6 TOP RAIL

4×4 POST

2×8 CLEAT

2×8 BEAM,
SECURE TO POST
W/ (3) ½" × 6"
GALV. BOLTS

2×8 BRIDGING

2×10 FASCIA

2×8 END JOIST
2×8 BEAMS, THROUGH-BOLT TO POST W/(3) ½"×8 GALV. BOLTS
4×4 POST

2×8
STAIR
PLATFORM
END JOIST

AXONOMETRIC/STRUCTURE

Courtesy of Southern Pine Council

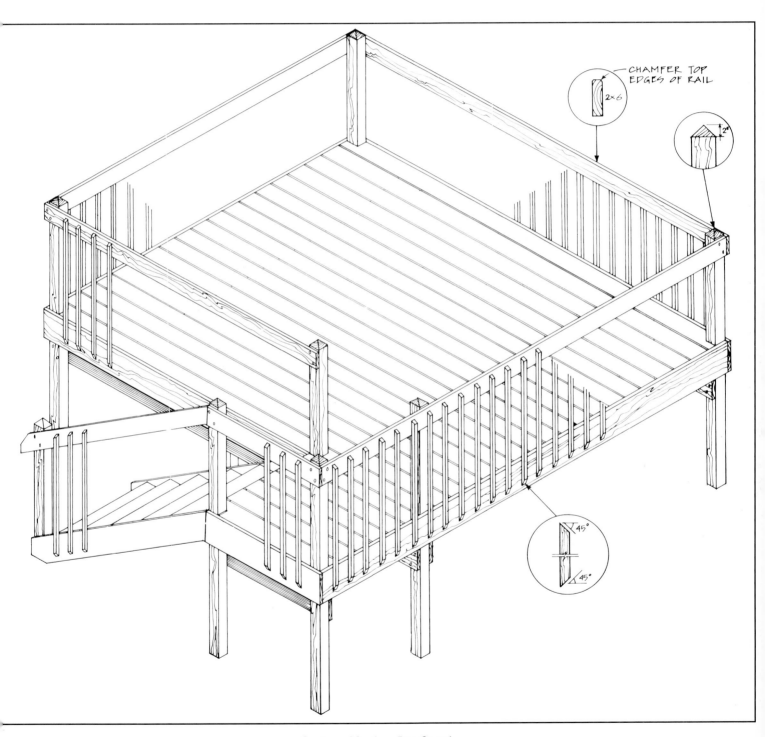

CHAMFER TOP
EDGES OF RAIL

2×6

2"

45°

45°

Courtesy of Southern Pine Council

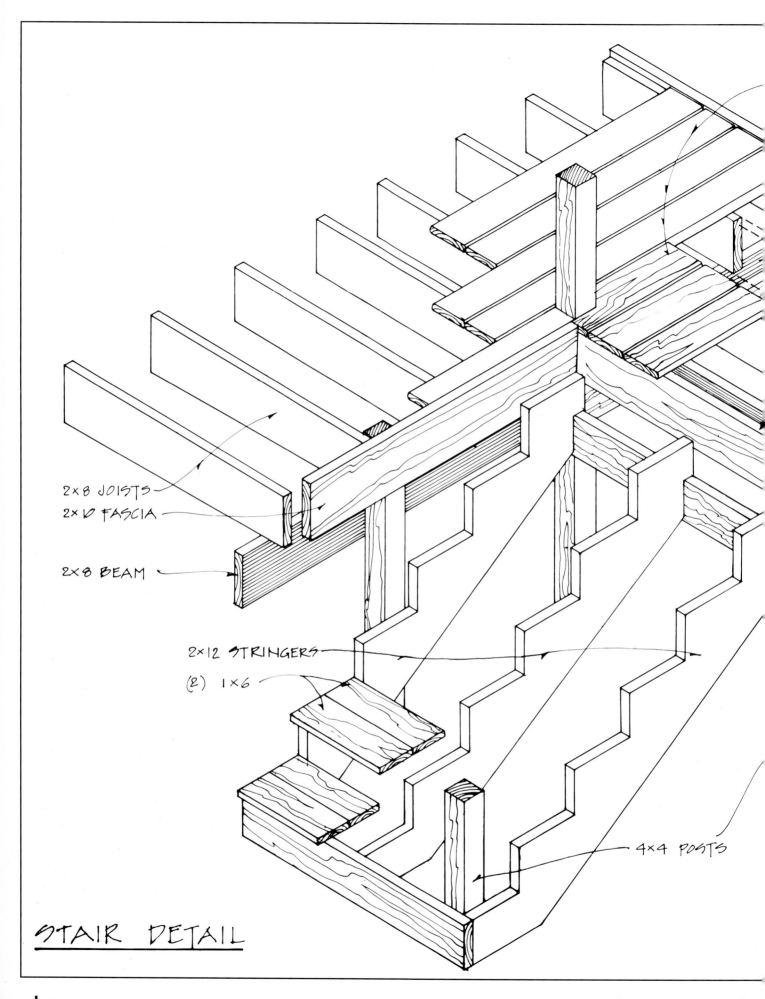

2×8 JOISTS

2×10 FASCIA

2×8 BEAM

2×12 STRINGERS

(2) 1×6

4×4 POSTS

STAIR DETAIL

110

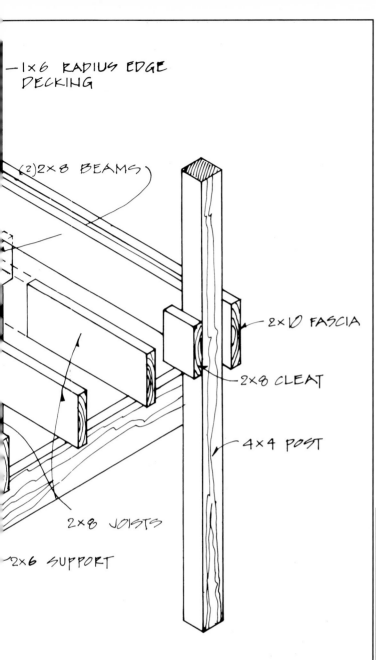

—1×6 RADIUS EDGE
DECKING

(2)2×8 BEAMS

2×10 FASCIA

2×8 CLEAT

4×4 POST

2×8 JOISTS

2×6 SUPPORT

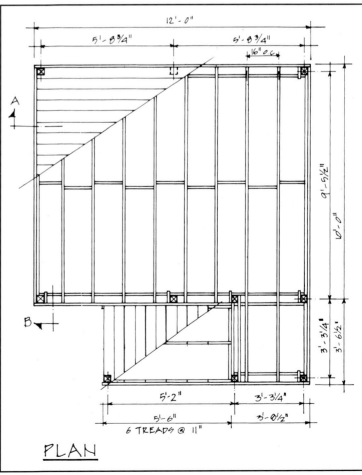

12'-0"

5'-8¾"   5'-8¾"

16" O.C.

A

9'-5½"

10'-0"

B

3'-3¼"

3'-6½"

5'-2"   3'-3¼"

5'-6"   3'-0½"

6 TREADS @ 11"

PLAN

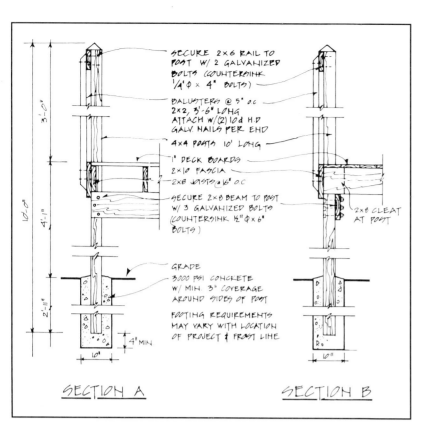

SECURE 2×6 RAIL TO
POST W/ 2 GALVANIZED
BOLTS (COUNTERSINK
¼" ∅ × 4" BOLTS)

BALUSTERS @ 5" OC
2×2, 3'-6" LONG
ATTACH W/(2) 10d H.D
GALV NAILS PER END

4×4 POSTS 10' LONG

1" DECK BOARDS
2×10 FASCIA
2×8 JOISTS @ 16" OC

SECURE 2×8 BEAM TO POST
W/ 3 GALVANIZED BOLTS
(COUNTERSINK ½" ∅ × 6"
BOLTS)

2×8 CLEAT
AT POST

GRADE
3000 PSI CONCRETE
W/ MIN. 3" COVERAGE
AROUND SIDES OF POST

FOOTING REQUIREMENTS
MAY VARY WITH LOCATION
OF PROJECT & FROST LINE

3'-0"
10'-0"
4'-1"
2'-11"
4" MIN
10"
10"

SECTION A   SECTION B

Courtesy of Southern Pine Council

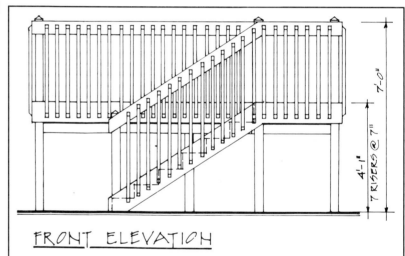

FRONT ELEVATION

7'-0"
4'-1"
7 RISERS @ 7"

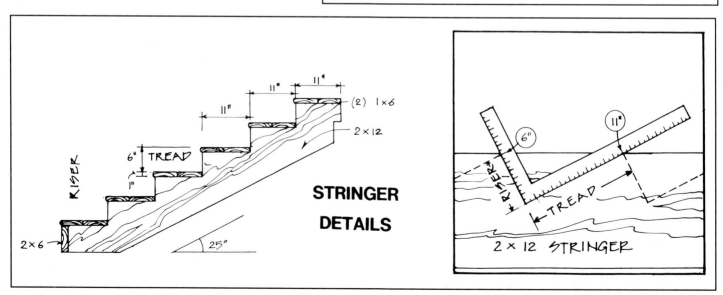

(2) 1×6
2×12

11"
11"
11"

RISER
6" TREAD
1"

2×6
25°

STRINGER
DETAILS

6"
11"
RISER
TREAD
2 × 12 STRINGER

Courtesy of Southern Pine Council